Saul Leiter

Introduction by Max Kozloff

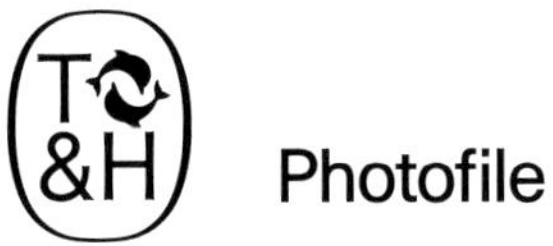

Photofile

Saul Leiter's Elegance

Saul Leiter told me that he has always found it comfortable to be ignored. For a creative personality, that attitude is today so outlandish as to be suggestive of an earlier age, when American artists were unprepared to handle success or notoriety and were ashamed of it. The period at issue would be the 1950s. However they might secretly long for acclaim from media, avant-gardists feared that it would compromise their resistant stance. Some poets, composers, and numerous painters regarded popular culture as incurably complacent and philistine. Leiter was on familiar terms with a group of these painters, second-generation Abstract Expressionists who showed at the Tanager Gallery, near where he lived. To the extent their difficult work was unacceptable to middlebrow culture, they thought they had a right to consider themselves failures, a term that enjoyed a certain prestige in their own circle. Though he originally came to New York to become a painter, Saul Leiter circulated as a photographer who, during the late 50s to the 80s, made his living by fashion assignments. For such magazines as *Elle*, *Nova*, and *Esquire*, he furnished stylish images at a very high level and frequently without qualms. With what one writer has called "his disdain for self-promotion," Leiter dismisses the idea that his personal street pictures, a great archive from the period, only now coming to light, have anything new or noteworthy to show us. This sincere opinion is mistaken. It is a survivor, not of modernist exceptionalism but of a belief quite the opposite—the modesty that Leiter feels when he compares himself with the old masters he reveres.

Nevertheless, even a casual look at the photographs in this book will convince readers that, far from being a traditionalist, he is in the forefront of photographic innovators, daring for his time and quite obviously, in ours. Fashion photographers may often have a bohemian side; Leiter is a bohemian who demonstrates mastery—and independence—in all genres. He shuffles the attributes and protocols of nudes, portraits, still life, and street work with such interchangeable versatility that a viewer often remains unsure of the genre at issue. This fluent miscegenation of picture norms is one of the most radical features of his work.

Why should a "detail" like the sole of a work boot (ill. 2), seen from an ant's viewpoint, have taken over the whole image, at the expense of the sidewalk? Why should furnishings have overly intruded upon a view of a lithe nude woman (ill. 36)? Either there is too little pictorial context, or it is made to look extraneous. Yet, rather than flaws of exposition, these aspects of Leiter's work mark the discoveries of his unusually inquisitive perception. He considers what lies underneath, is off to the side, or gets in the way of his nominal subject. He juggles foreground and background indiscriminately, such that they trade places—to surprising effect. As for elusive story content, it is deflected by his taste for the sheer, distracting potpourri that is New York experience. The outcome of his seemingly perverse reconfigurations is at the same time unfamiliar and everyday. "Depend on it," said Sherlock Holmes, "there is nothing so unnatural as the commonplace."

Holmes, of course, was a compulsive sleuth, whereas Saul Leiter is a poetic *flâneur*. Yet, who would have thought there was so much mystery available to his roving eye? Three men wearing hats walk by, two toward our left, one the other way (ill. 3). In this chance cluster, a leg that stretches down to the bottom right is obscured at the knee, which makes us uncertain as to the direction it is going, let alone the person to whom it belongs. A view of his foot would be enlightening, but it is withheld. In a charming fashion shot (ill. 61), we can't decide if the hands that grip the mannequin next to the live model are plaster or are made of flesh. If he had to select between what we think we see, and what the camera actually confirms in a split second, no matter how inexplicable, the photographer chooses the latter. One of his characteristic motifs is a lattice (ill. 21) whose vertical glass panels break up the reflected street into discontinuous segments, like a pocket map that can't be refolded. However unruly they may at first appear, things are given a new logic by the rhythms and accords created for them within the frame.

The 1950s was a flammable and conflicted moment in the history of New York photography. There was as yet little consciousness of the medium as an art form, though many of its practitioners had serious intent. They certainly knew their marvelous European precursors, Henri Cartier-Bresson, André Kertész, and Lisette Model. And they were able to draw upon a native documentary heritage, which had waned at the activist Photo League but was flourishing at the cosmopolitan Magnum photo agency. Alexey Brodovitch, the fashion art director, had circulated his influential book on ballet, a eulogy to blurred bodies in action. William Klein, an American expatriate from Paris, visualized a gritty capitalist New York, berserk with signs. Saul Leiter worked in parallel with Robert Frank, but he was closest in spirit to Lou Faurer, an elegist who regarded the city as a maze of half-lights and faded hopes. Leiter shared many of the themes developed by these colleagues in a volatile environment, but his form is much more apparitional. Where they sometimes evoked the "second life" of shadow and vagrant movement, he insisted upon it, as a matter of principle. Had passersby looked in the direction he pointed his camera, they would have been puzzled, for they would have seen nothing. His art consisted in making virtual events out of what appeared to be nothing in particular.

Rather than scenes, what we have instead are settings, populated décor. The incidents Leiter catches with the lens are generic and recessive, almost lost in his accent on the most specific phenomena of light, contrast, interval, and tone. Figures are treated as shapes before they are recognized as peddlers or readers of newspapers. It is a world of echoes and ricochets, observed from angles that emphasize the flatness of miscellaneous presences in the urban space. Meanwhile, the grey scale of black and white film helps to camouflage the distinction between chiaroscuro and substance, allowing incessant after-images to breathe in their own atmosphere. Over and over, he needs to render even shapeless phenomena in the form of palpable tones. To the extent after-images might interrupt the dialogue of forms, or seem to come from another domain, so much the better. Take, as an example the well-known picture of a man, seen from the back as he sits in a diner (ill. 6). Outside, the photographer's dark shadow reflected by the window brings out the white profile of the man's face, and, at the same time, a coffee mug with an up-ended spoon handle, located on a counter between them. The image starts out as a street shot, then is transformed into a still life, while at the same time it exists as a meditation and equally as a gesture. Leiter had to be exceedingly mobile to capture such abrupt quietude. Perception is not necessarily more acute when its conscious object is on the move, any more than when the one who perceives is active. But in the work of Saul Leiter, keenness of perception on just those terms, is everything. With a touch as light as chiffon, he visualizes a city suspended in its purposes, yet filled with subliminal import.

This was his vision of neighborhoods or vignettes in black and white; he practiced also with color, from his personal vantage, but with different results. Among photographers who roamed the streets of New York during the 1950s, Saul Leiter seems to have used the camera as a thermometer just as much as an optical instrument. This extra function is insinuated by his pioneer chromatic work, which records the city through screens of evidently disparate temperature zones. From where he stands, often in the shade, to what he sees, the centigrade level is not the same. Beyond his own locale, he likes snow, and does not mind a downpour of rain. His pleasure takes comfort from the implication of its own physical — and imaginative — shelter (ill. 15). He makes of umbrellas a lyric spectacle. One notices his enjoyment of the downy texture or foamy substance when selected passages are out of focus. A viewer can't tell when a pane of glass acts like a mirror or a cloth. One of his favorite topics is moisture that condenses by heat changes on windows (see ill. 33, for example), which smear the contours of objects and people. Visibility and climate affect each other in ratios of loveliness. Saul Leiter takes their measure as if he savors the airy weight of the environment itself, and not least, its variable influences on the body.

Yet, when he recreates the city's complexion, he orchestrates elements within the frame much more tightly than in his black and white photographs. (Partly this was a necessity imposed by the slower film speed of the color material.) Instead of thrusting his camera into activities about to fly apart or drift away, he relishes putting them together, with studied nonchalance. The instant of attention must account for the new sensory caprices that color brings into the field. Had he been a composer, the bass would be represented by his color chords, announced by signs, the treble by filigrees of light and nuance, in different, modulated hues. Each of his color images has a key signature, usually in the minor. I refer to his grays, lilacs, umber greens, lavenders, and brown oranges, all combined with a certain reticence and in low contrast. The muted quality of this palette does not correspond very well with the received popular notion of the city's harshness.

It is impossible to imagine the grate of sirens or arguments in this tranquil world of surfaces, where faces make cameo appearances, each lost in its own moment. The sensory roughage of New York life is softened and appears miraculously more coordinated in Leiter's art than it was in reality. Every motion seems decelerated, accessible to the reverie of an outside observer who immobilizes the flicker and smudges of behavior within the authority of the frame. The photographer approaches the city very freshly at the same time as he endows it with a certain patina, filtered through an historical retrospection that seems more European than American. His pictures of elevated train platforms, scheduled to be torn down, have a nostalgic glow about them. He's fond of antique lamp-posts, balustrades, pawn shop windows, and vendor's carts. When revealed in color, they seem dusted with a tender recognition of their age. Just as there are after-images in his oeuvre, these are remainders from an earlier metropolitan scene. Here, the low-keyed chromaticism has a symbolic function, for it overlays a feeling for the past upon an urban environment that is otherwise contemporary. Not only do we have the weight of atmosphere in these images, but the weight of memory.

Yet, even in this backward look, he introduces a new variant—his use of a telephoto lens. Telephoto is an ambiguous ingredient in the construction of scenes. Well known for its planar emphasis in the transcription of depth, it leaves the actual spatial relationship of the seer to the seen open to question. No longer can we count on mid-distance as a transition to events that would have been perceived as further away. Intermediate territory either drops out or is at best only a hypothesis within the field. The telephoto lens engenders a vague, compressive, and deceiving proximity, favorable to Saul Leiter's decorative instincts. It also enables him to suggest the privacy of his sensations. In this strange mix of voyeurism and detachment, passersby act only as sentient foils to the intersection of things and reflections.

These New Yorkers are often shunted to the margins of a spectacle that is half like a poster and half like a dream. They exist in an urban-scape made up of just bits and pieces that have little in common but their amputation by the frame. The only view one image gives of a passenger on the subway is that of his foot, resting on a wicker seat (ill. 56). His shoe is a well-polished example of its kind, but it is really its placement that makes it elegant. Before he can be said to care for them as objects of use or as social beings, the photographer treats his subjects as motifs.

Each photograph takes on its life through a reflexive distribution of motifs. It would be more accurate to call this distribution "pictorial" in the ontological sense than as an attribute of style. Instead of an aperture through which the gaze is directed, Saul Leiter conceives of the street photograph as a field upon which forms are visualized as if on a screen. (The fact that he used slides, positive transparencies, might relate to this impression, for they had to be projected on a screen.) If it had been horizontal, the 35 mm oblong view would have encouraged a reading from right to left, suggestive of story. These vertical images, contrarily, oblige the eye to scan upward and down within a slim area. Such confinement makes you notice how pressure along the sides energizes the field within, how the opportunistic framing creates absences, in order to enhance presences.

All the while, Leiter continues to paint gouaches that he's never publicly shown. They hover between landscapes and abstraction in a manner reminiscent of French symbolist art, the school of Pont Aven, with Gauguin at its head, and the Parisian Nabis. Had this New Yorker been transported to their era, he would have been glad to meet Atget and Vuillard. As it is, some recollection of their work, improbably fused, comes back to us in the photography of an American who pictured a very different world. He gives to it a translucence we never knew it could have had, colored by the assurance and yet also, the delicacy of his witness. Let us hope that this shy artist became reconciled to the admiration that was belatedly and justifiably bestowed upon his art.

Max Kozloff

This essay is a modified and expanded version of an article that appeared in the Spanish magazine Matador, 2006.

"Leiter is a rare artist, one whose vision is so encompassing, so refined, so in touch with a certain lyrical undertone, that his best photographs occasionally seem literally to transcend the medium."

Jane Livingston, *The New York School*

1. Umbrellas, c. 1947.

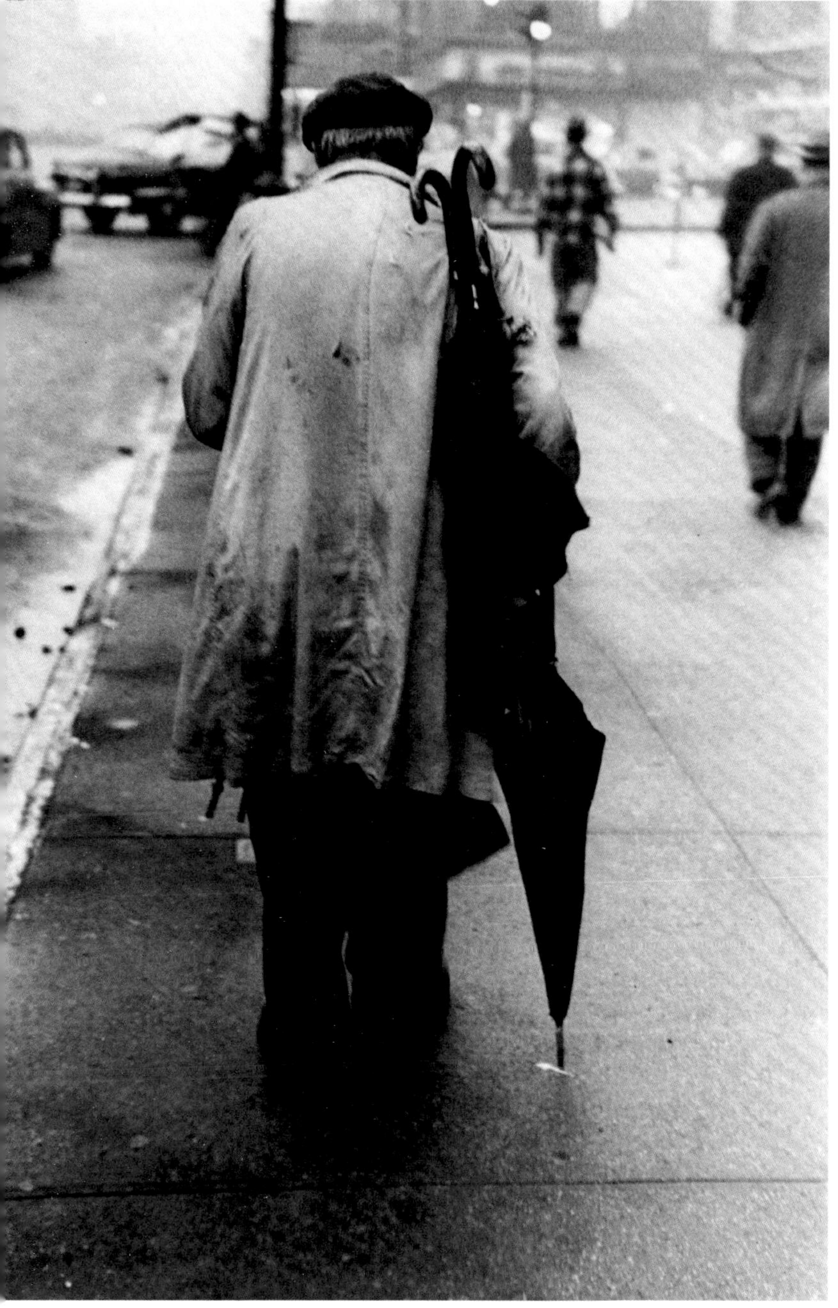

2. Shoe, c. 1951.

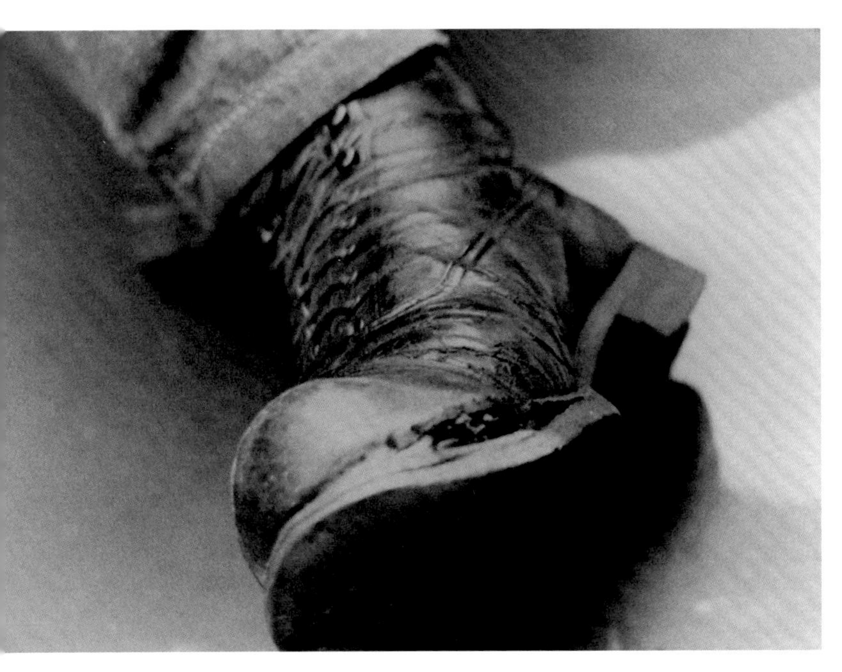

3. Hats, c. 1948.

Overleaf:
4. Hats, c. 1958.

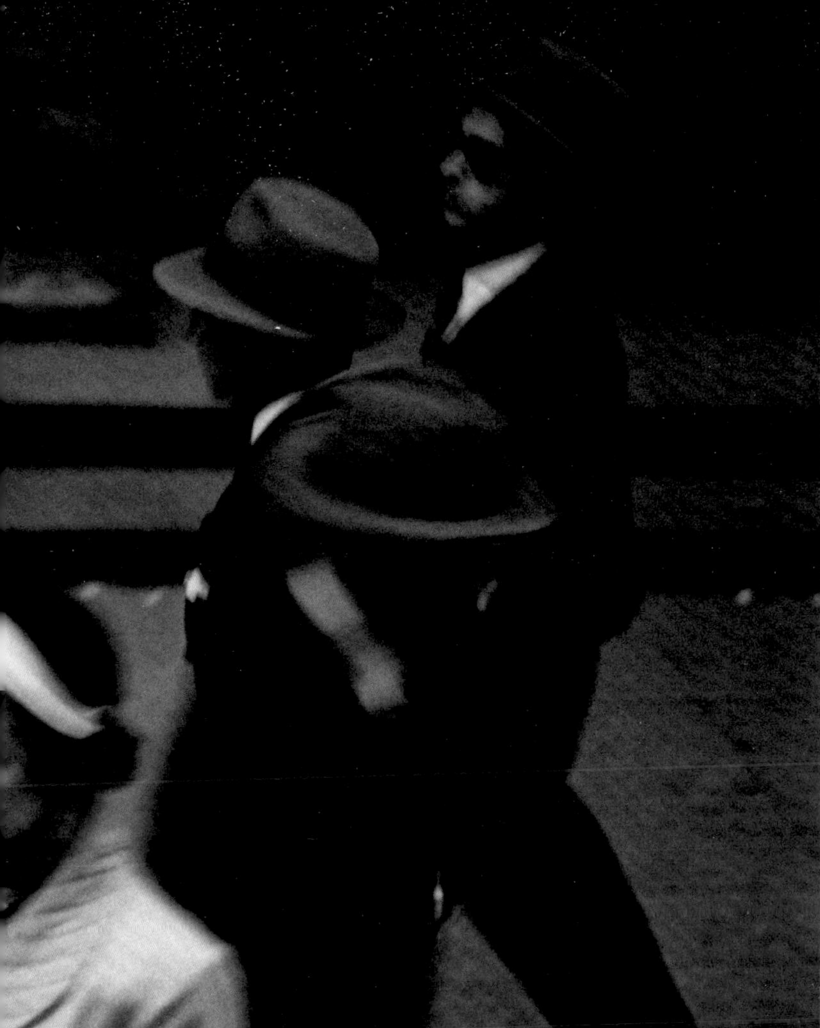

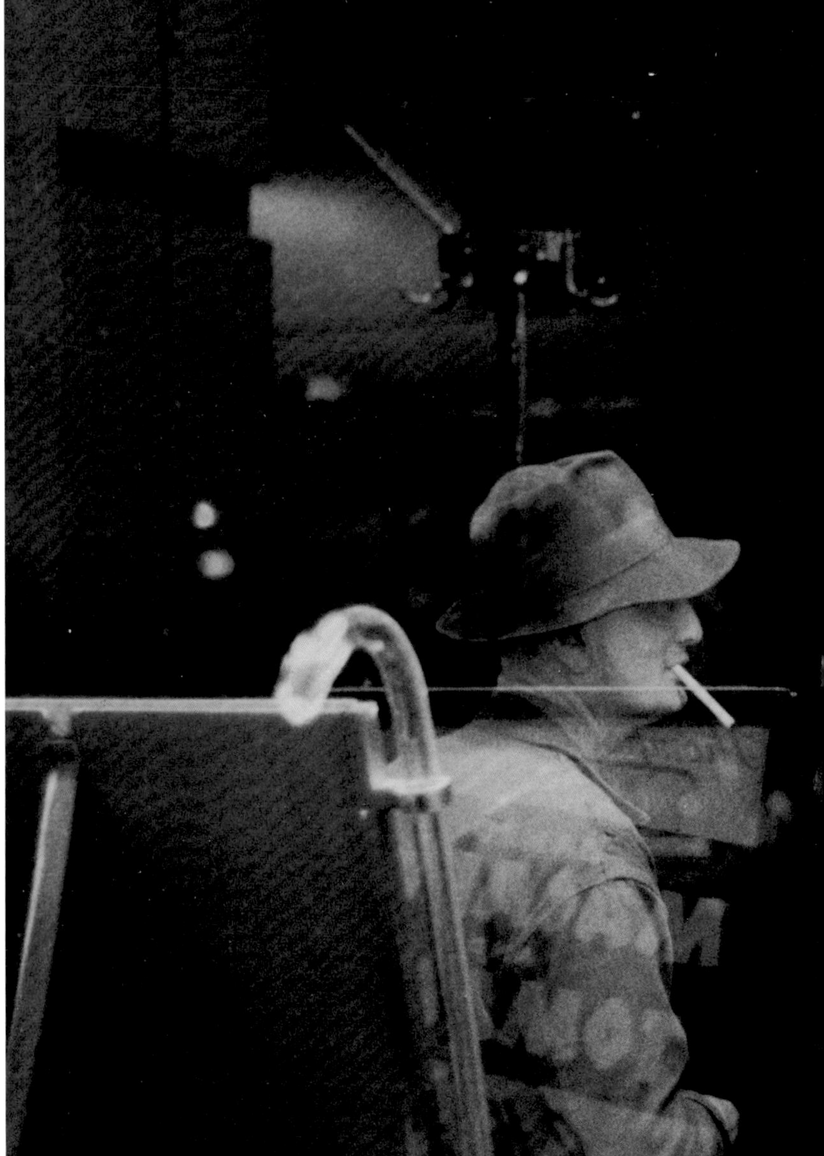

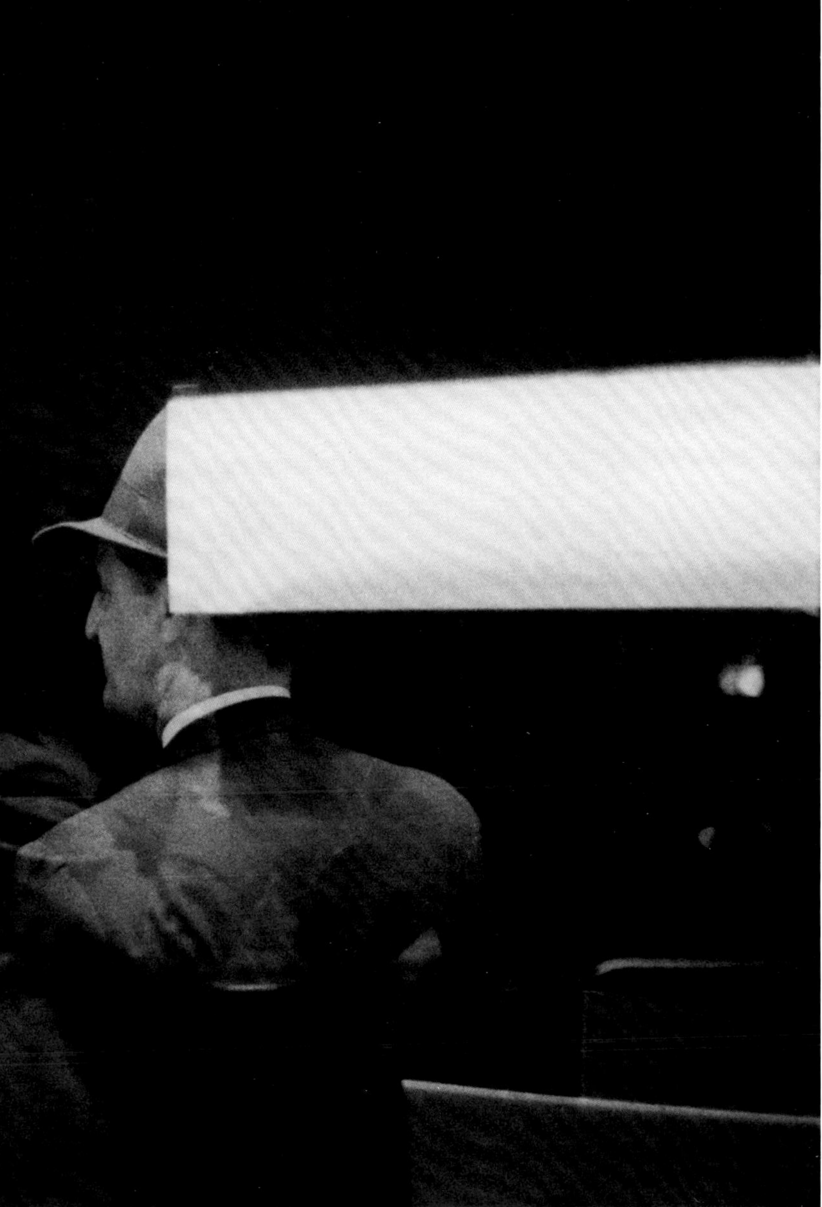

5. Wind, c. 1953.

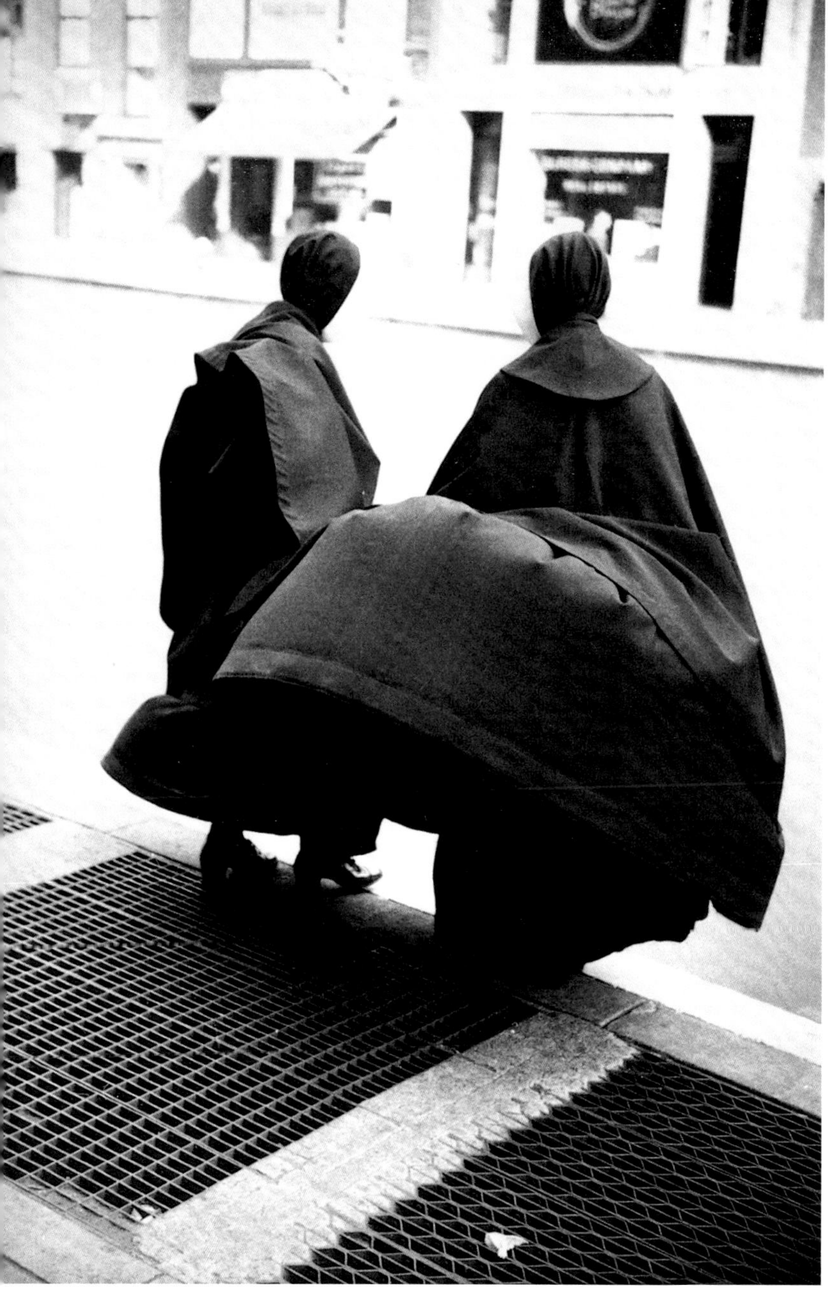

6. Self-portrait, c. 1952.

Overleaf:
7. Mary, c. 1947.

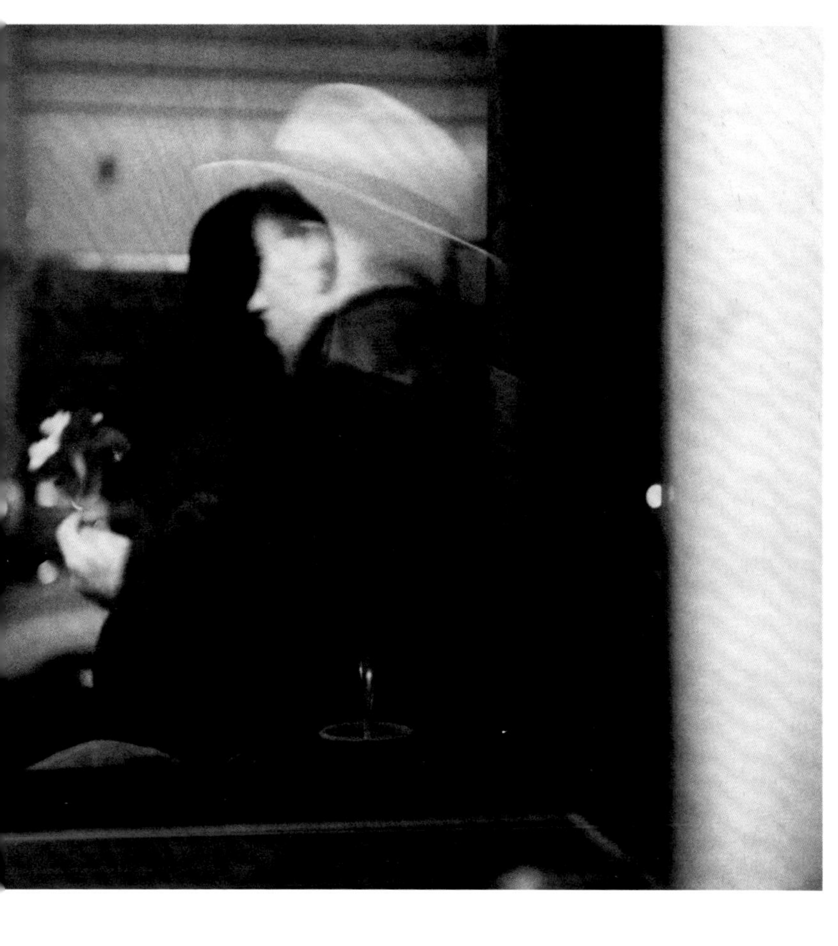

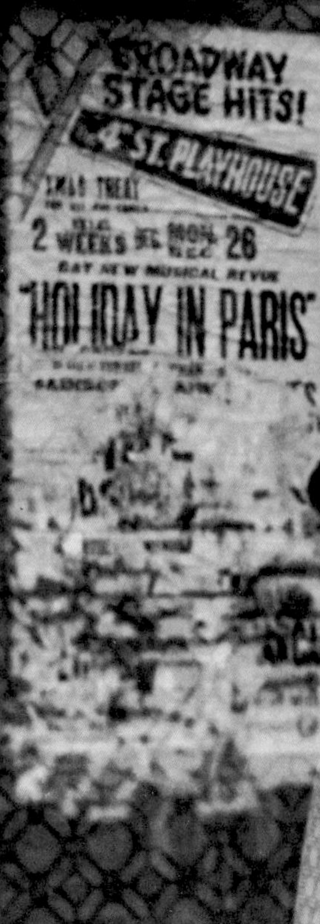
BROADWAY
STAGE HITS!
ST. PLAYHOUSE
"HOLIDAY IN PARIS"

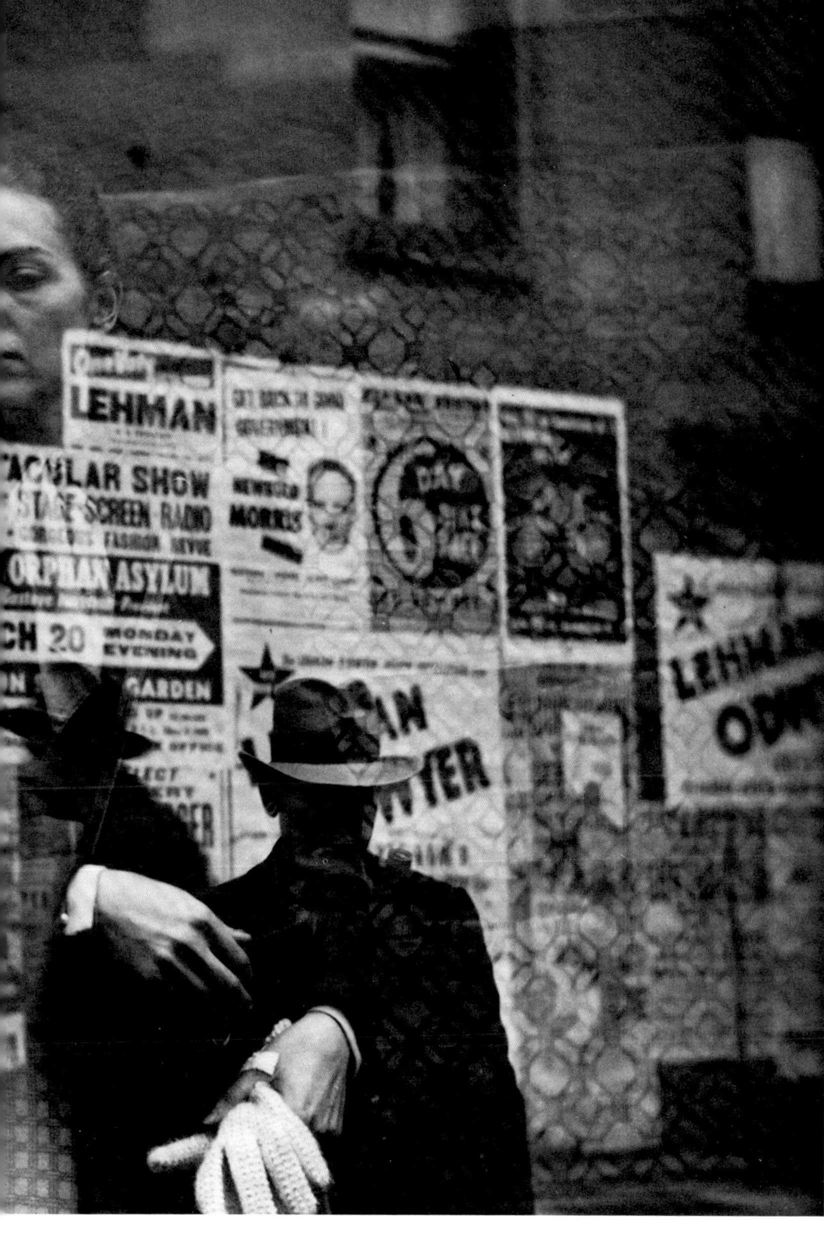
LEHMAN
TACULAR SHOW
STAGE-SCREEN-RADIO
FASHION REVUE
ORPHAN ASYLUM
CH 20
MONDAY EVENING
GARDEN
NEWBOLD MORRIS
DAY
LEHMA

8. Halloween, c. 1948.

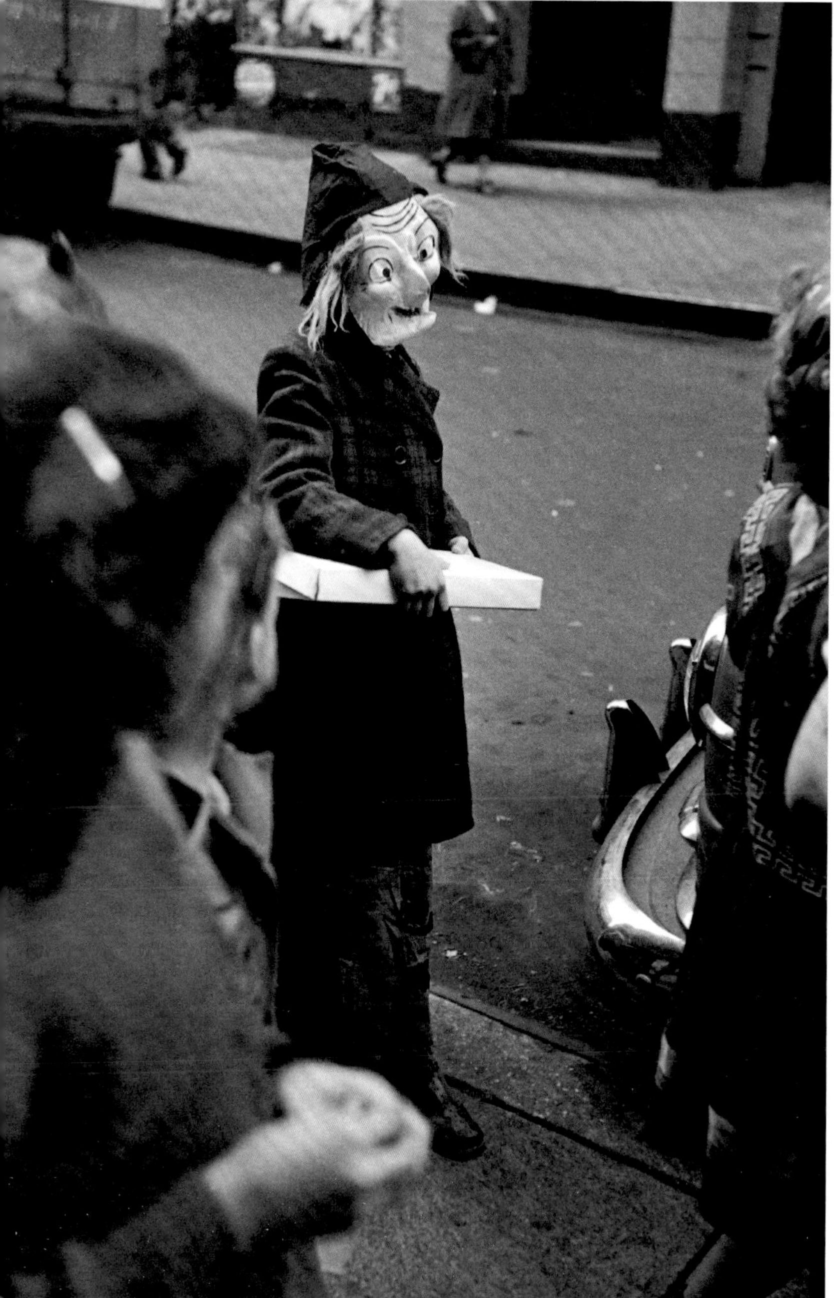

9. White circle, c. 1958.

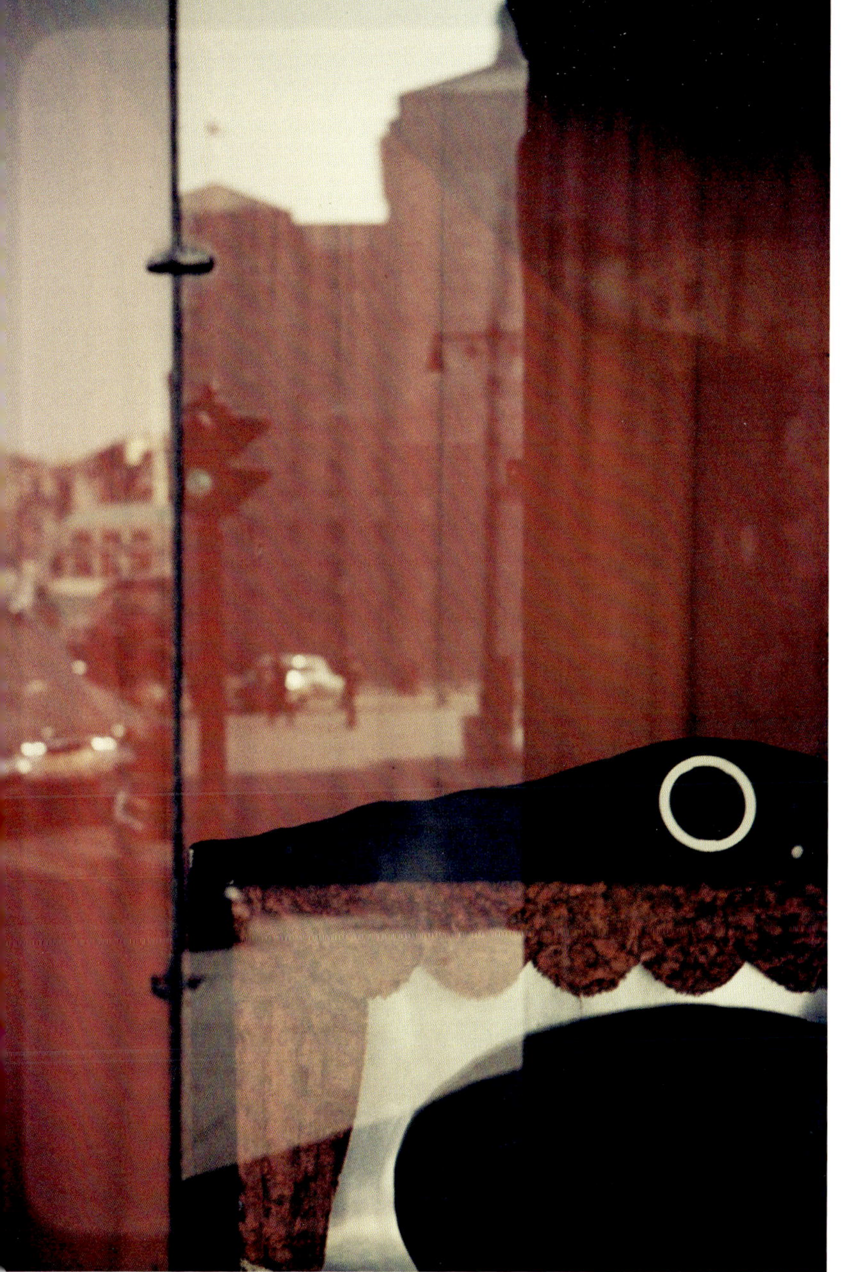

10. Store, Second Avenue, c. 1953.

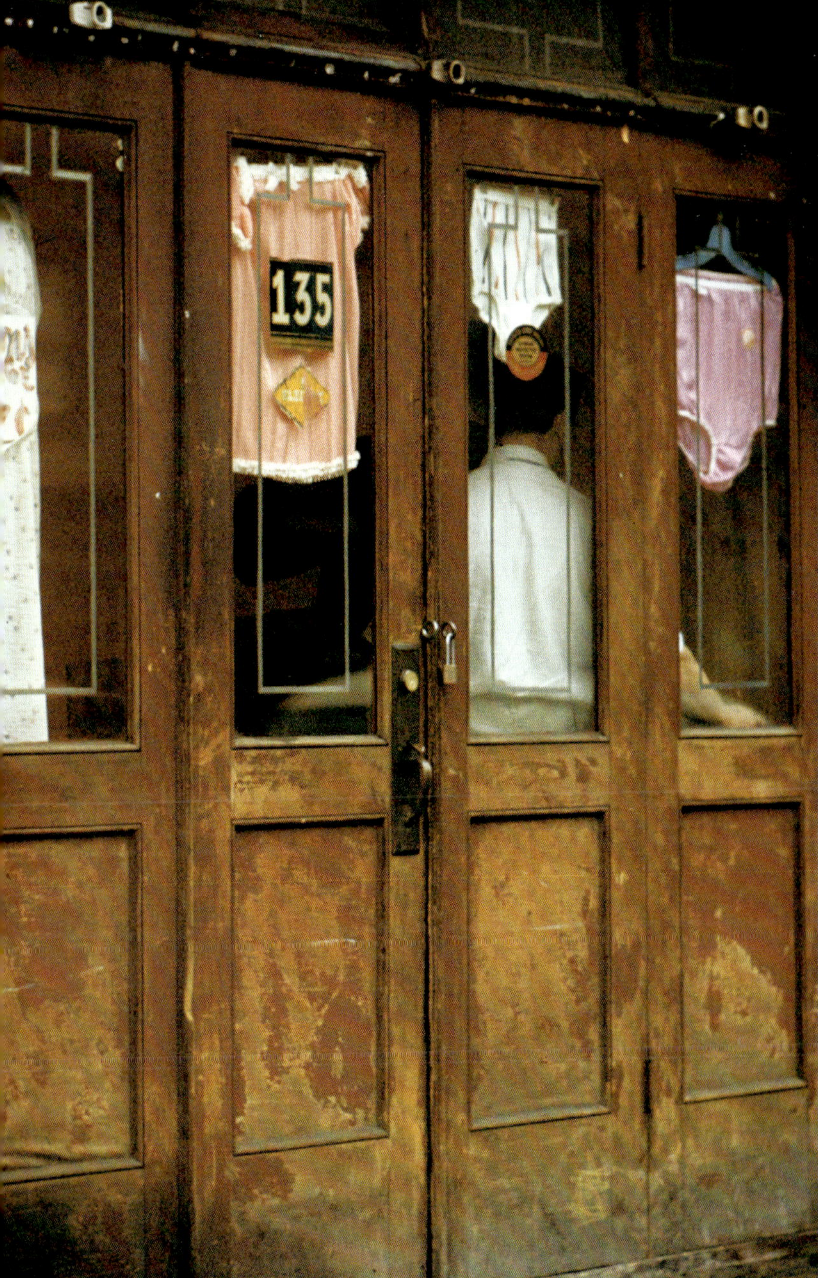
135

11. Elaine's, c. 1958.

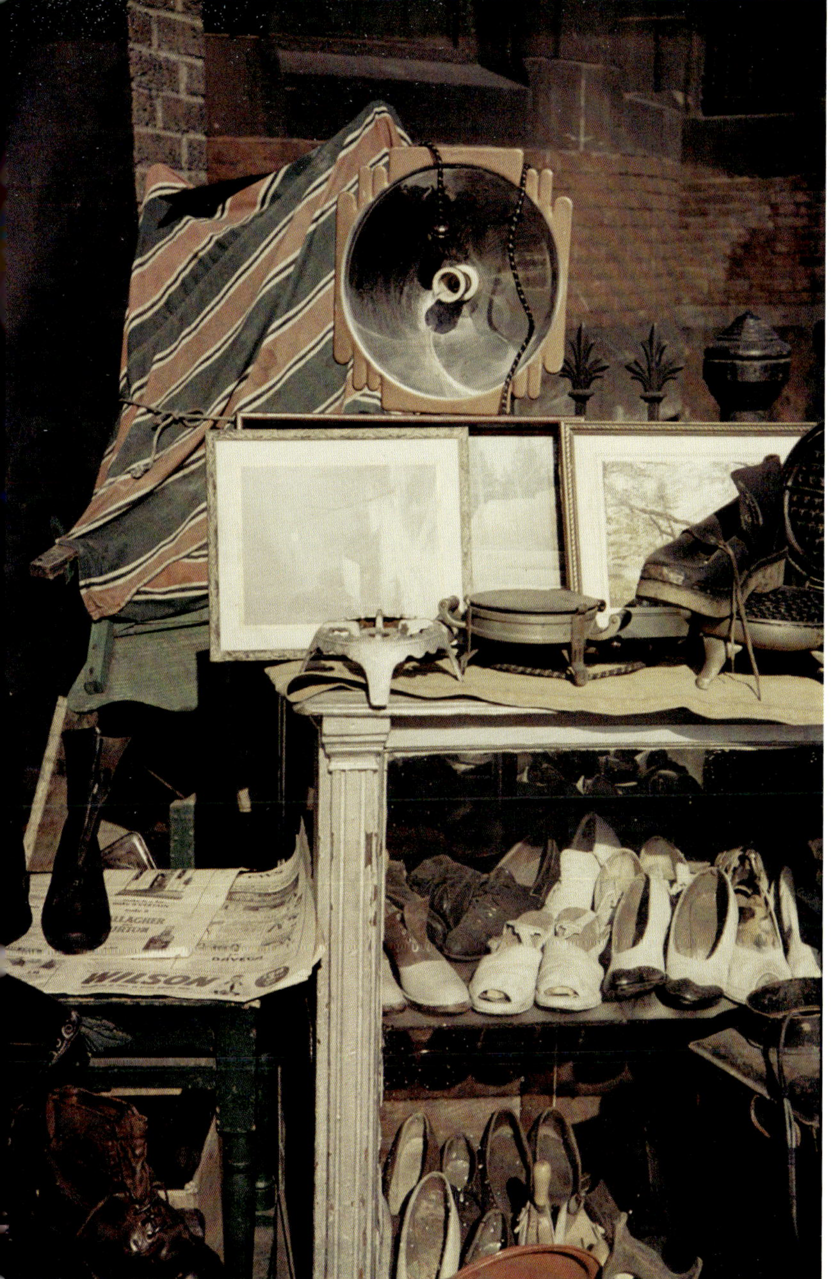
WILSON

12. Shoeshine, c. 1954.

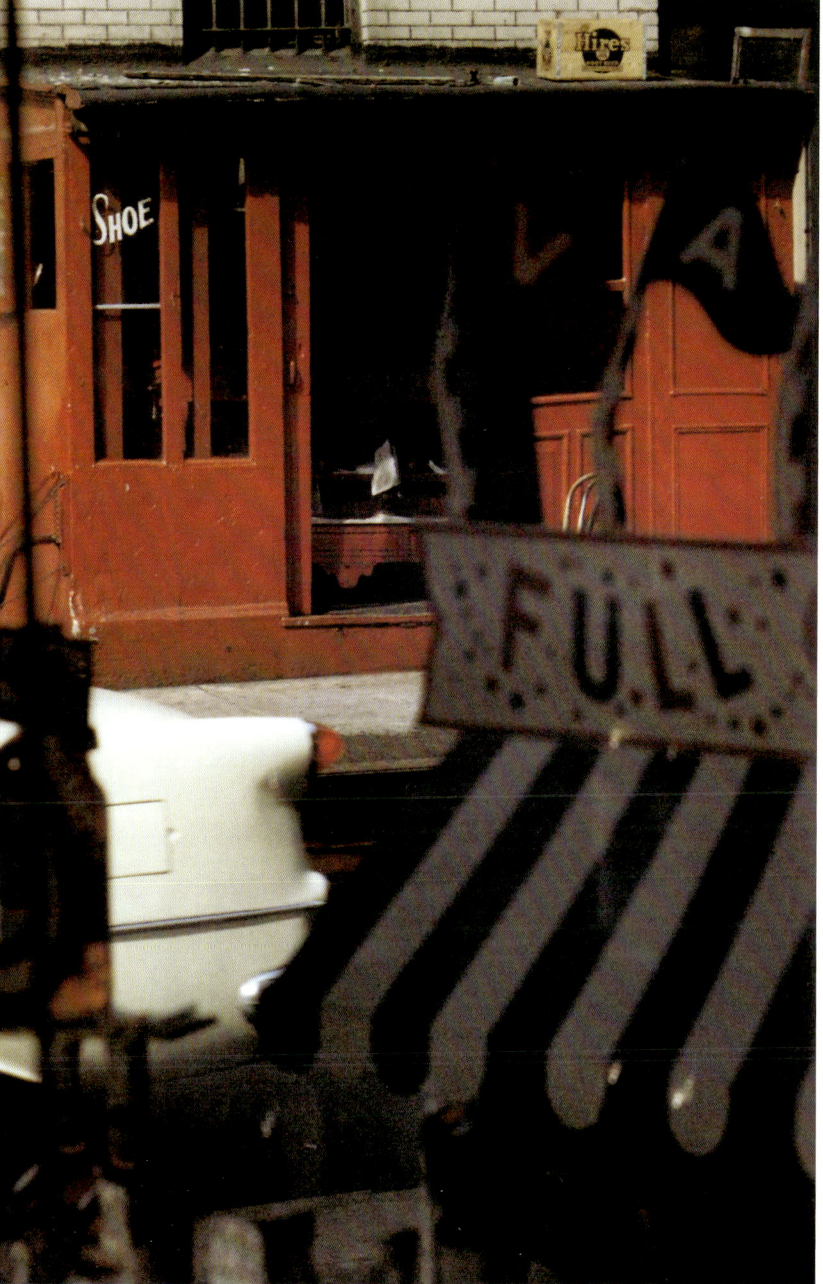
Hires
SHOE
FULL

13. Reflection, 1958.

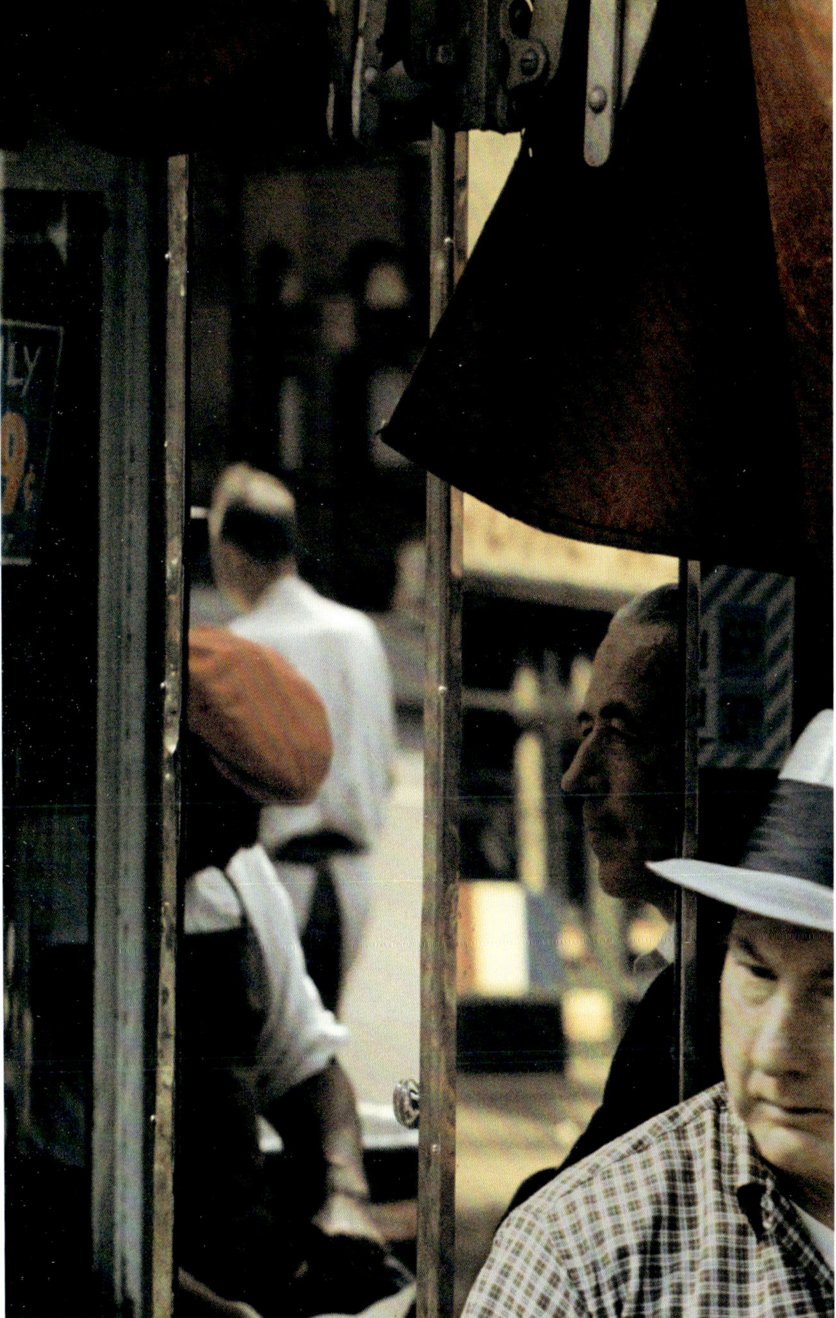

14. Postmen, c. 1952.

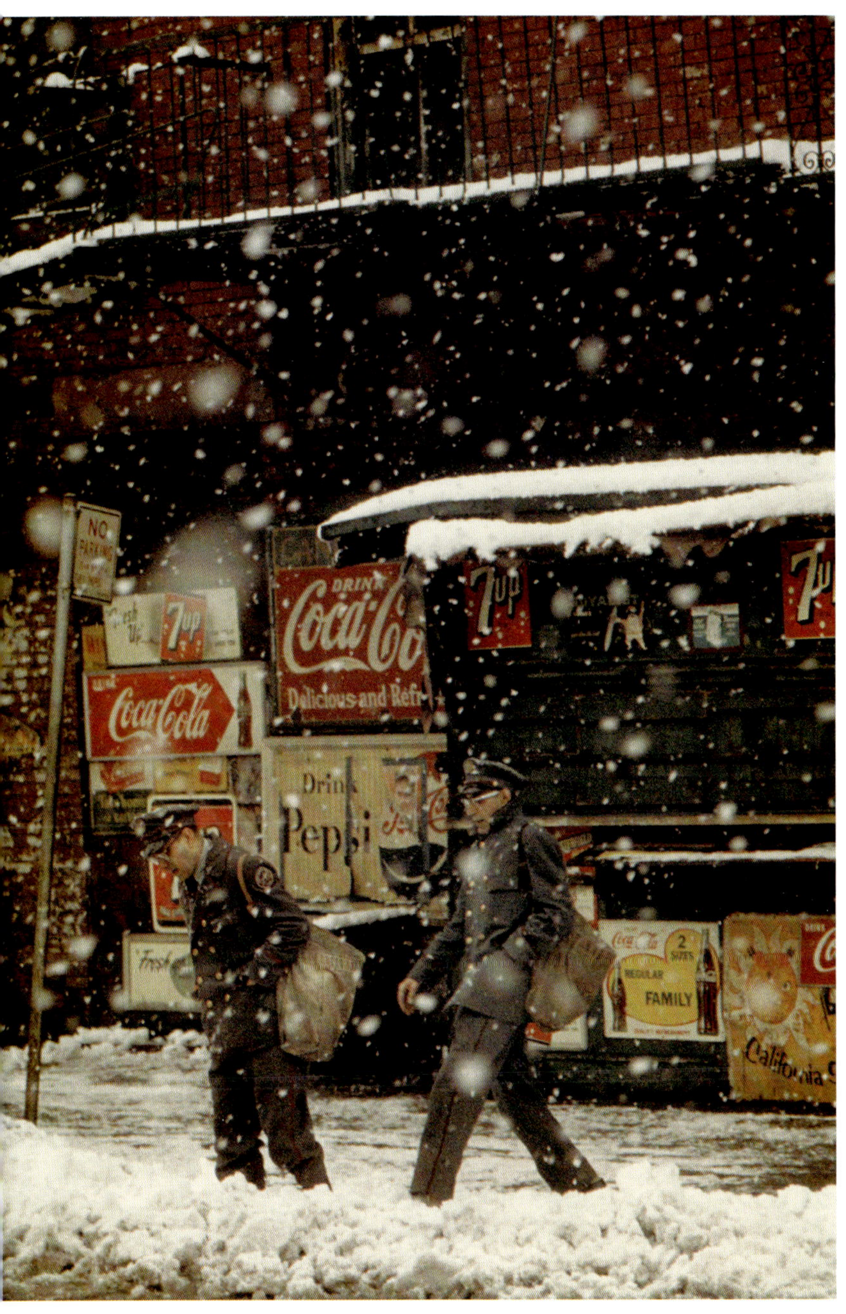

NO
DRINK
Coca-Co
Delicious and Refr
7up
7up
Coca-Cola
Drink
Pepsi
2
REGULAR
FAMILY
California

15. Canopy, c. 1958.

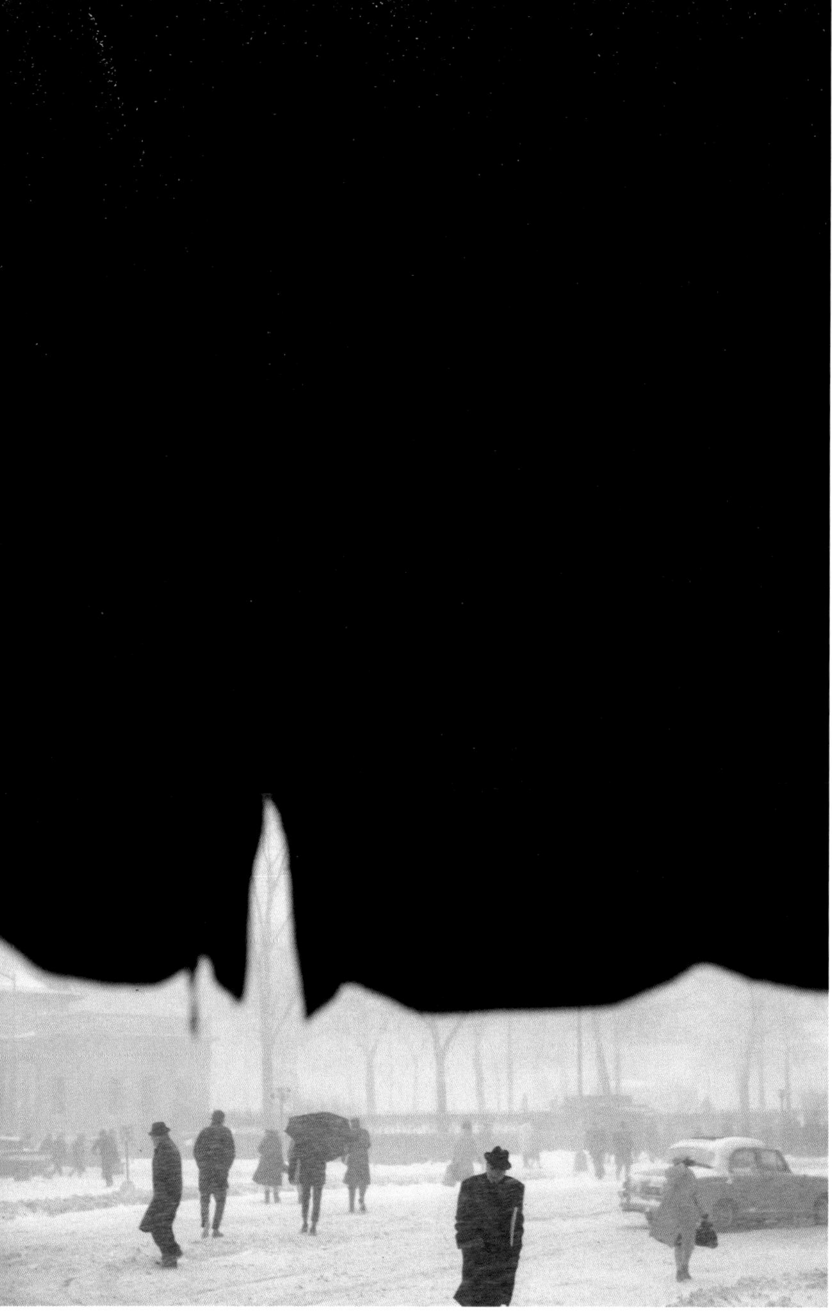

16. Green light, c. 1955.

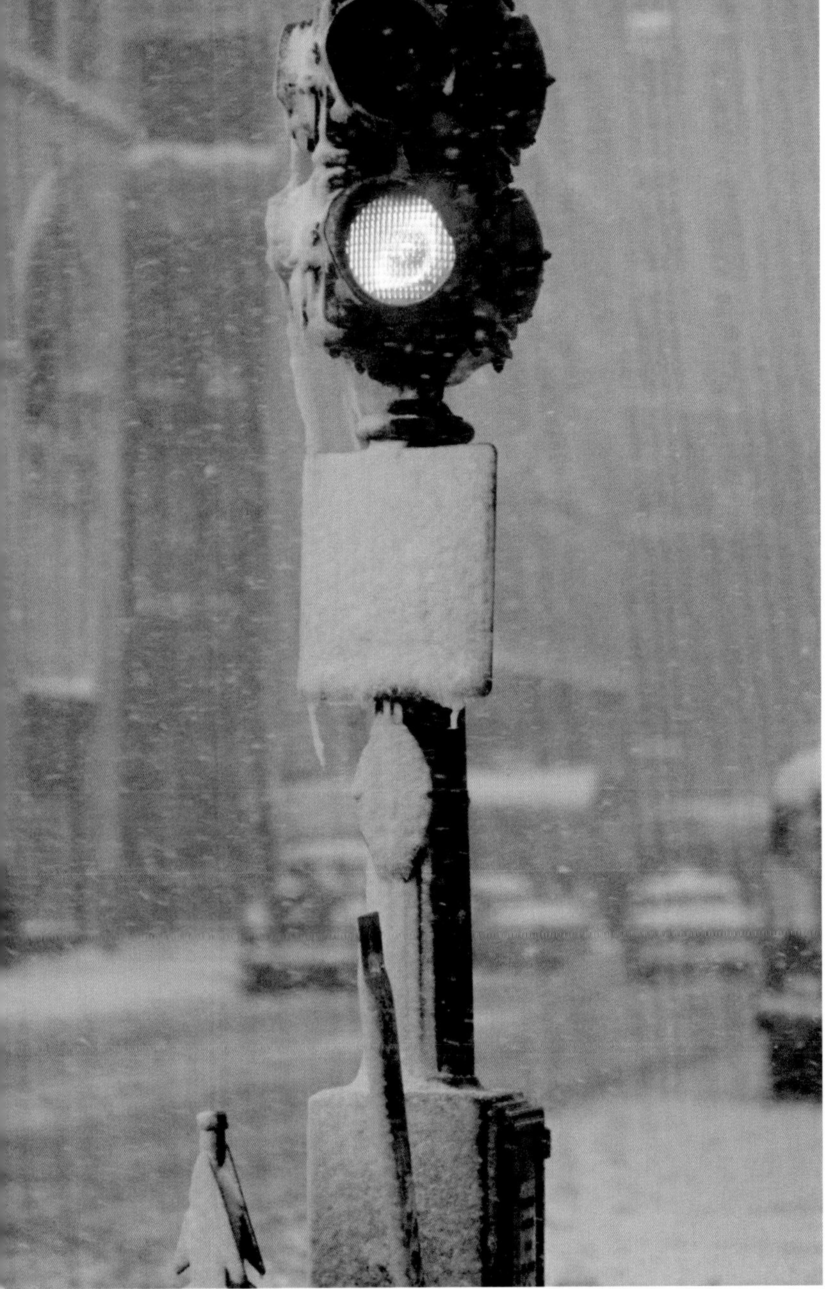

17. Red umbrella, c. 1957.

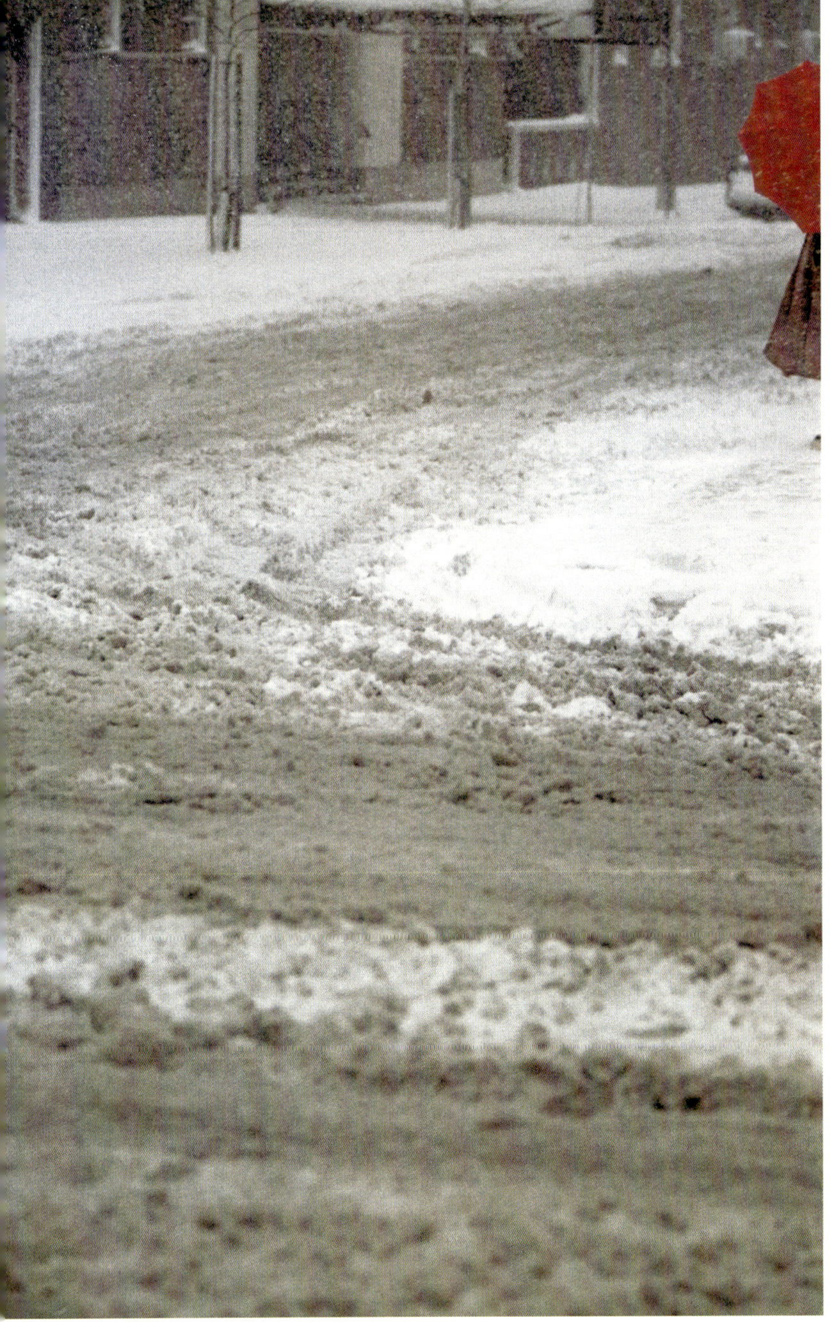

18. Snow, 1970.

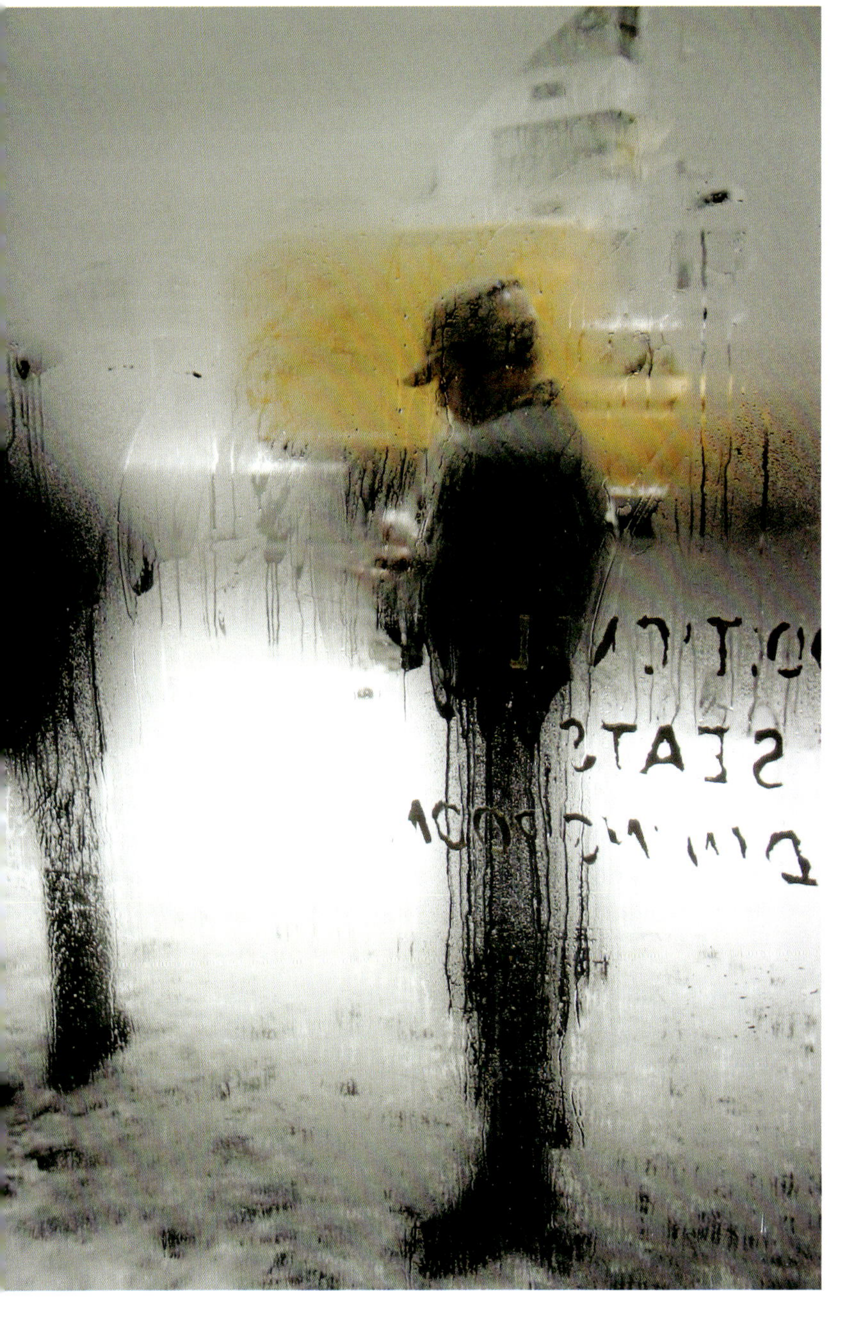

19. Pipes, c. 1960.

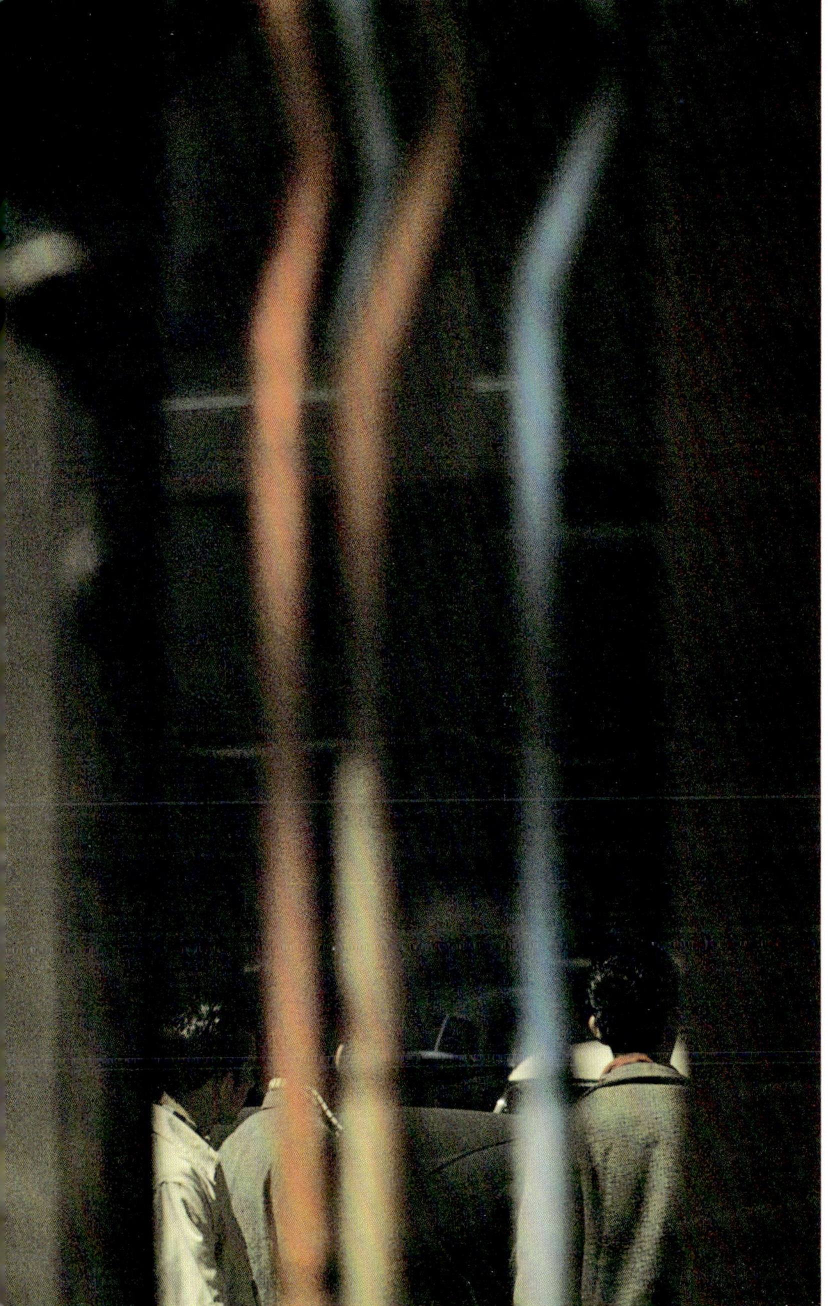

20. Red curtain, 1956.

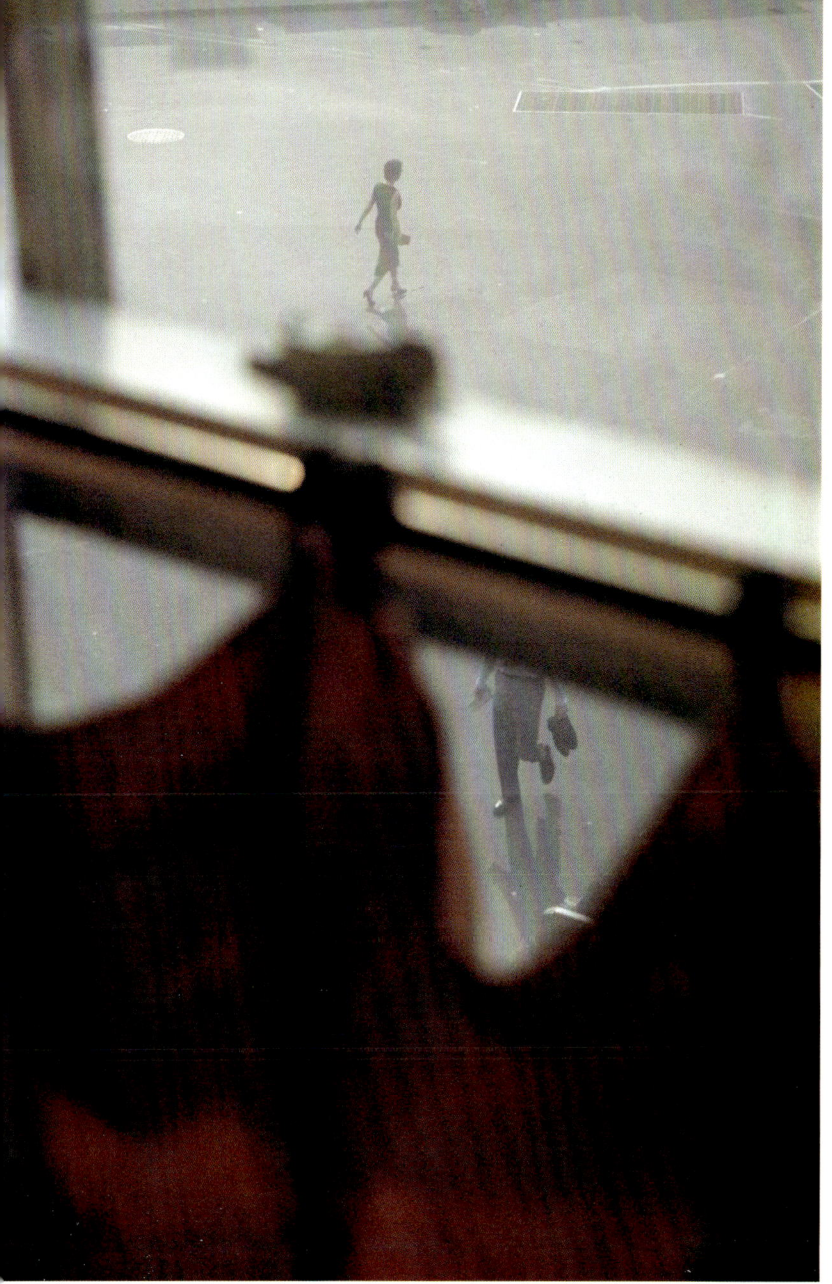

21. Mirrors, c. 1958.

22. Harlem, c. 1960.

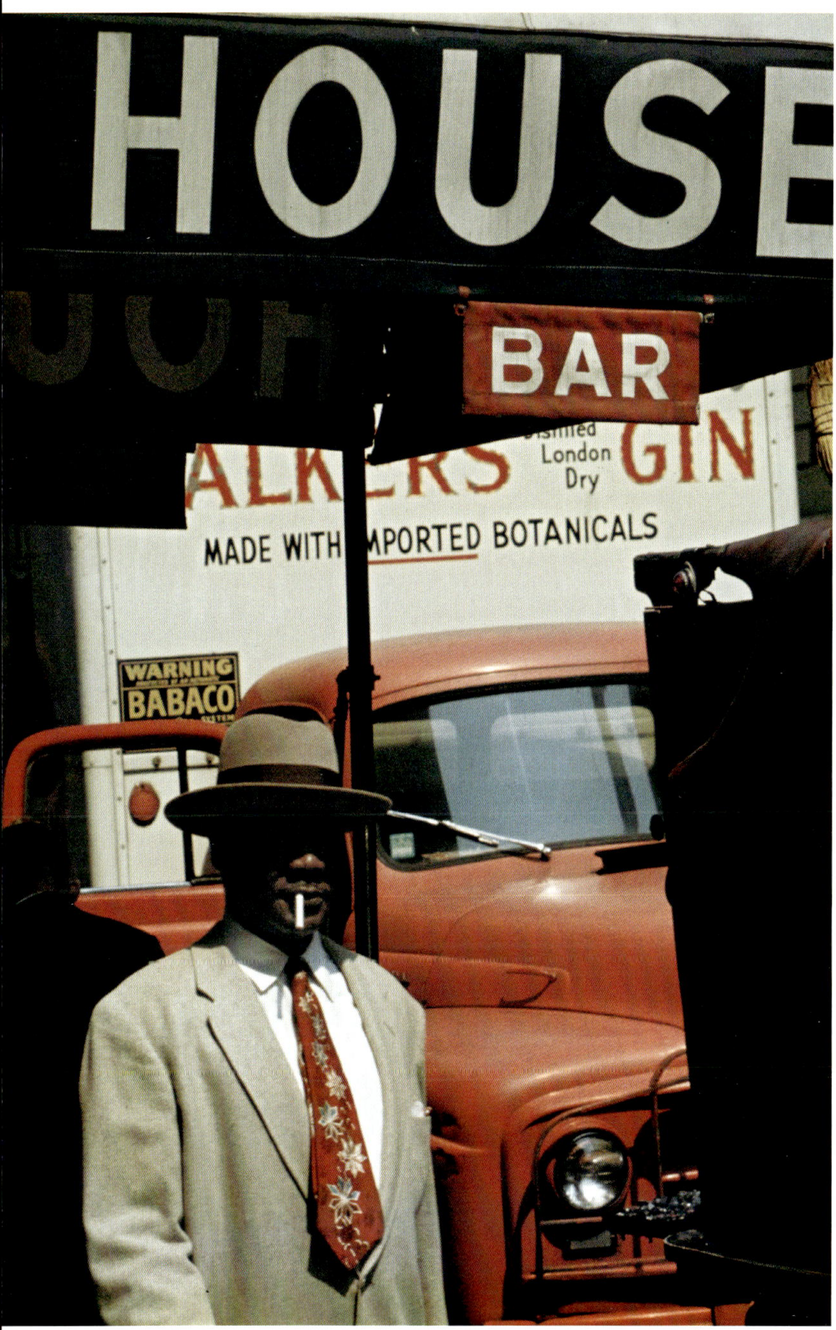

HOUSE
BAR
ALKERS
London
Dry
GIN
MADE WITH MPORTED BOTANICALS
WARNING
BABACO

23. Man on ladder, c. 1954.

Overleaf:

24. Phone call, c. 1957.

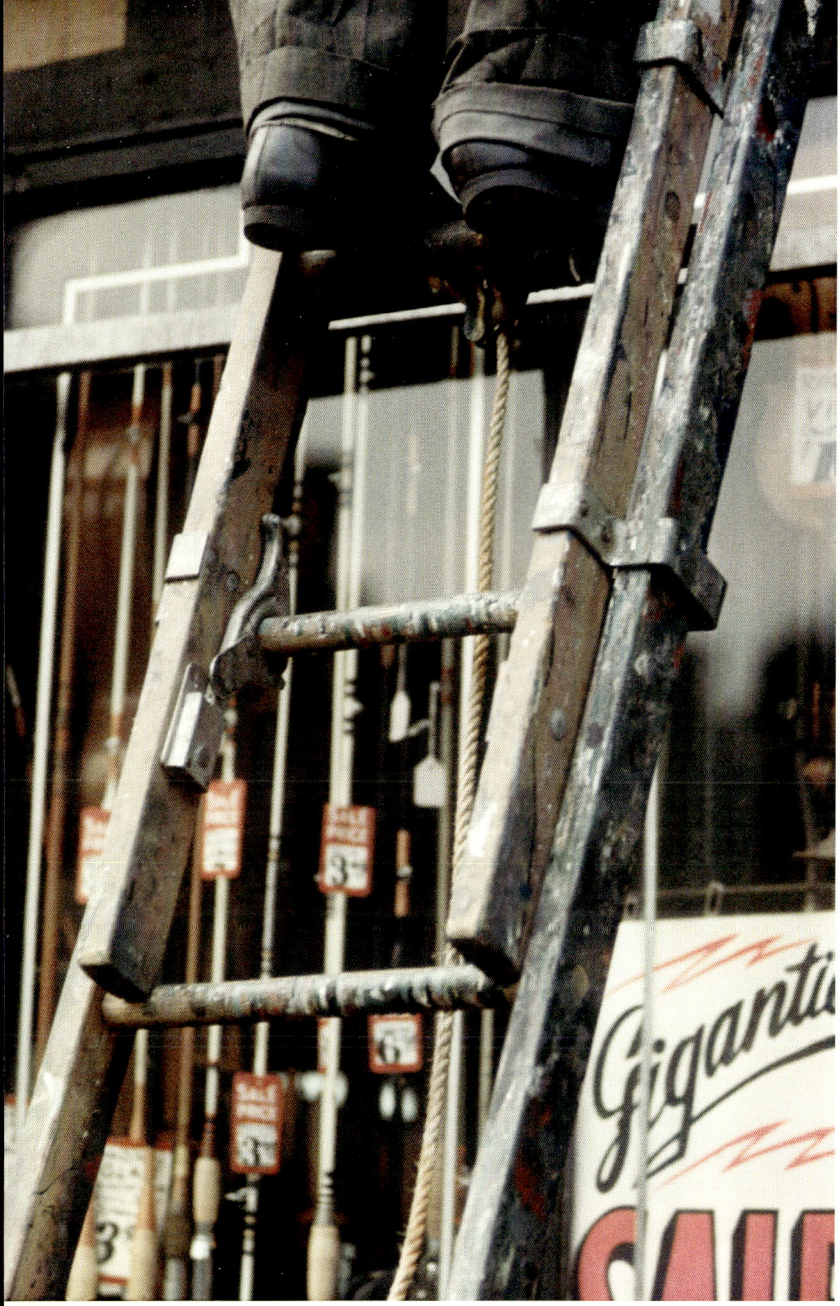
Giganti

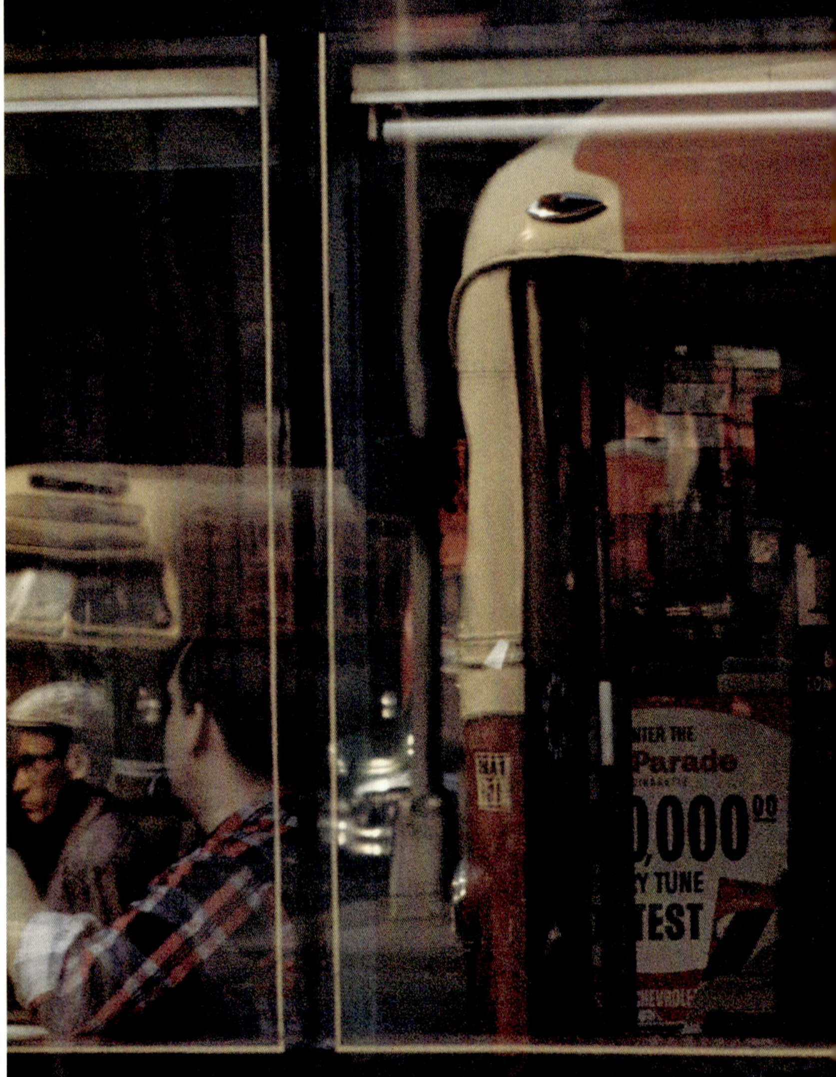
NTER THE
Parade
0,000 00
Y TUNE
TEST
UBLIC T

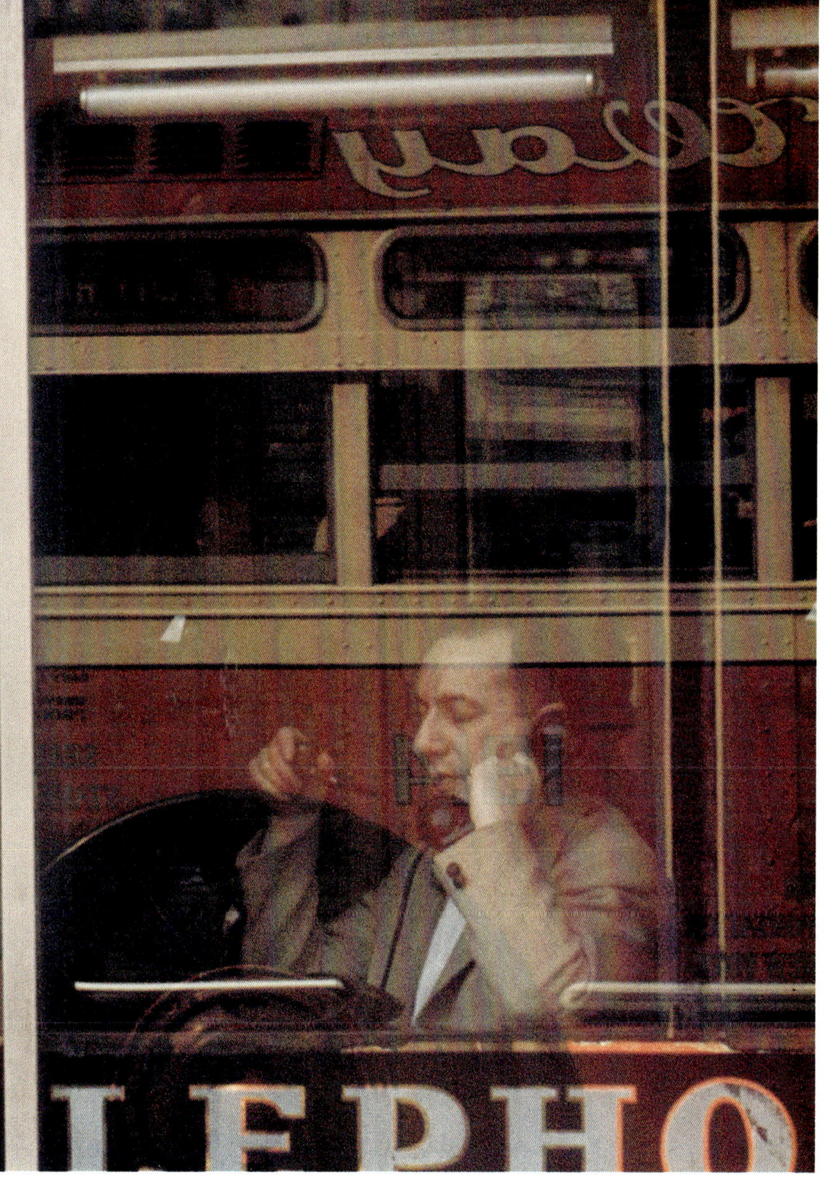
LEPHO

25. Straw hat, c. 1955.

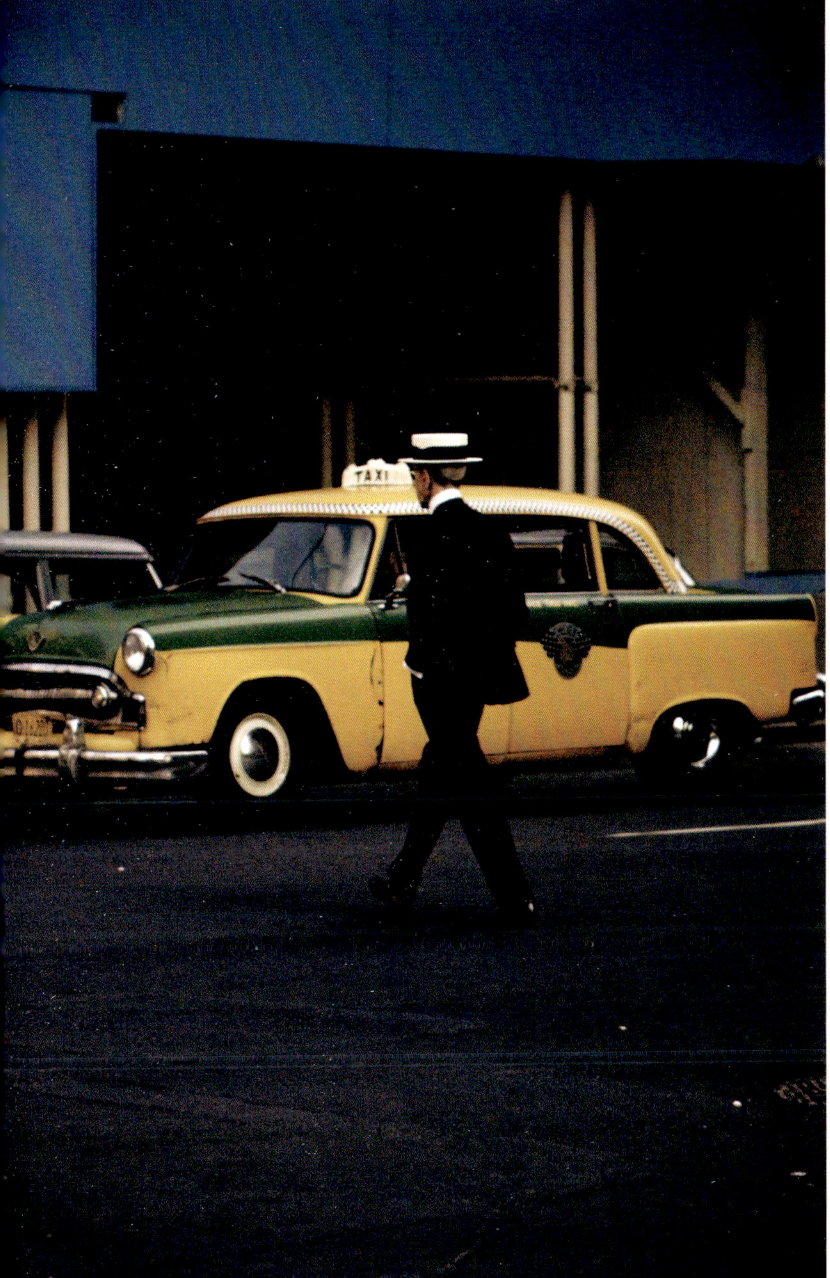
TAXI

26. Taxi, c. 1956.

Overleaf:

27. Taxi, 1957.

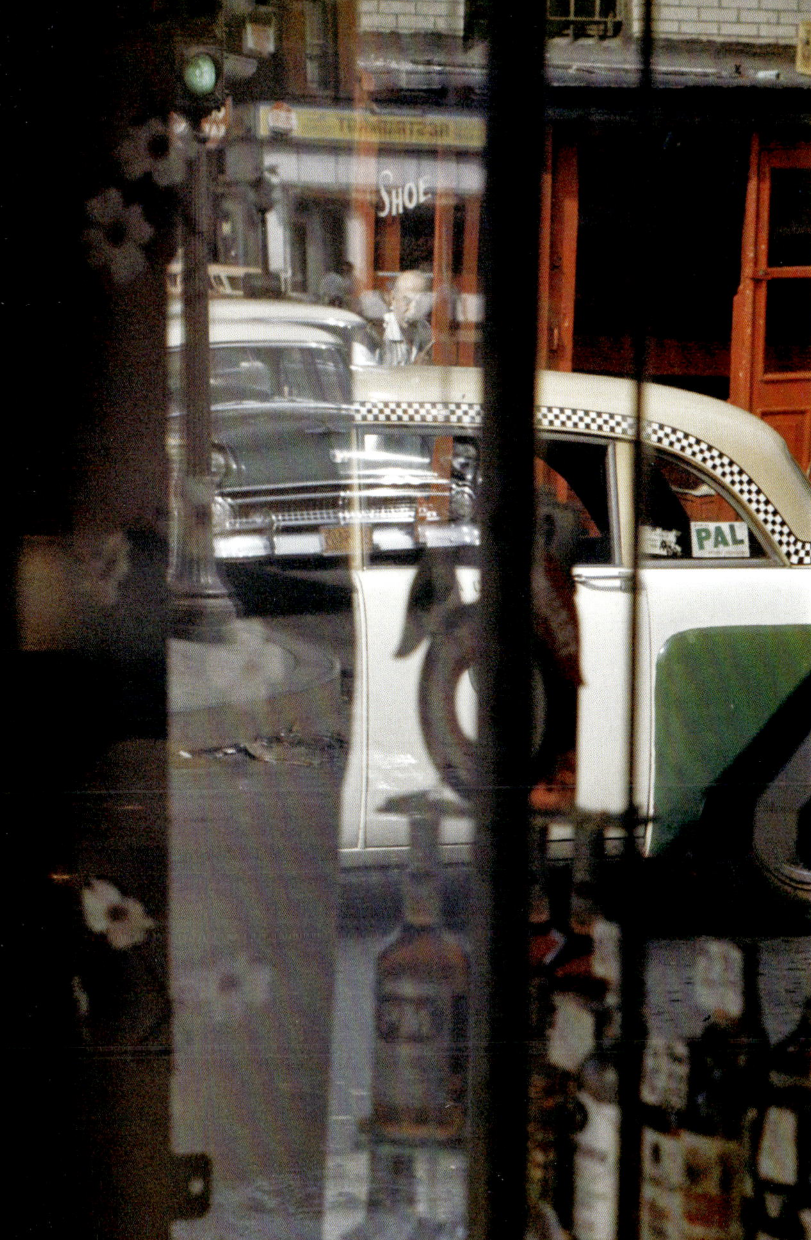
SHOE
PAL

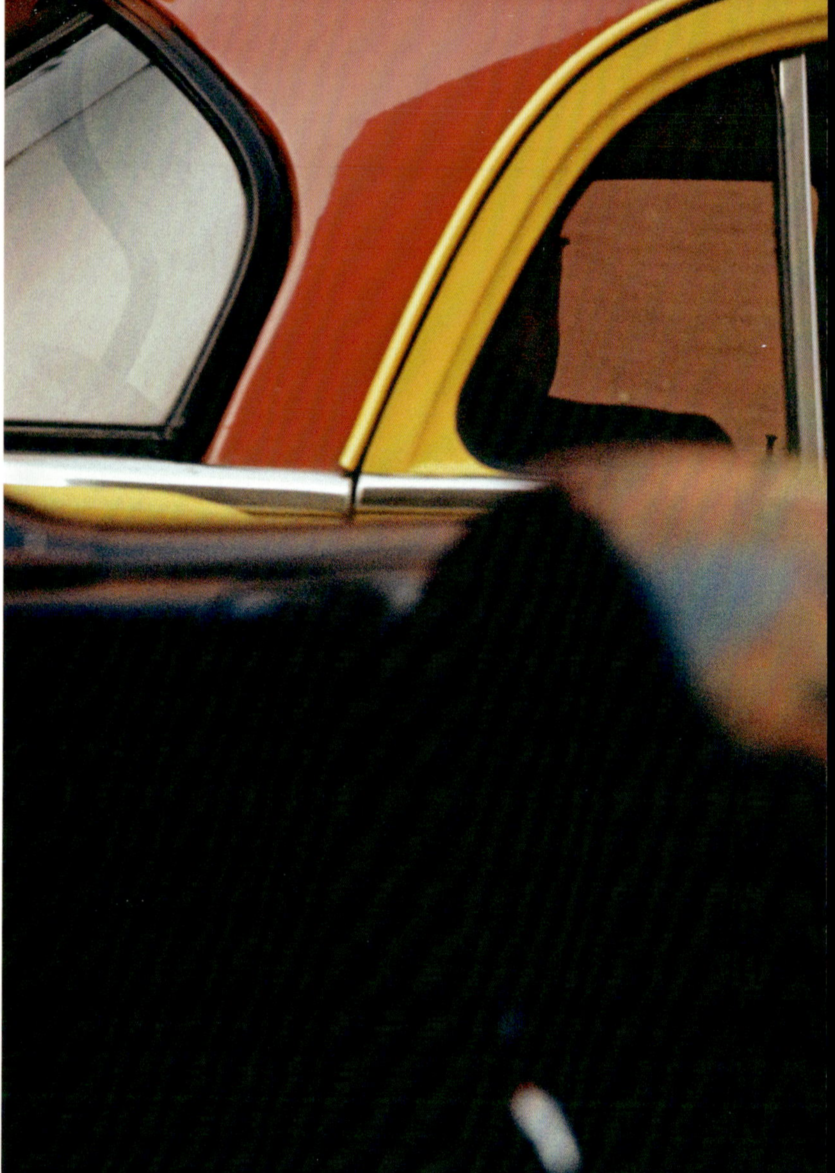

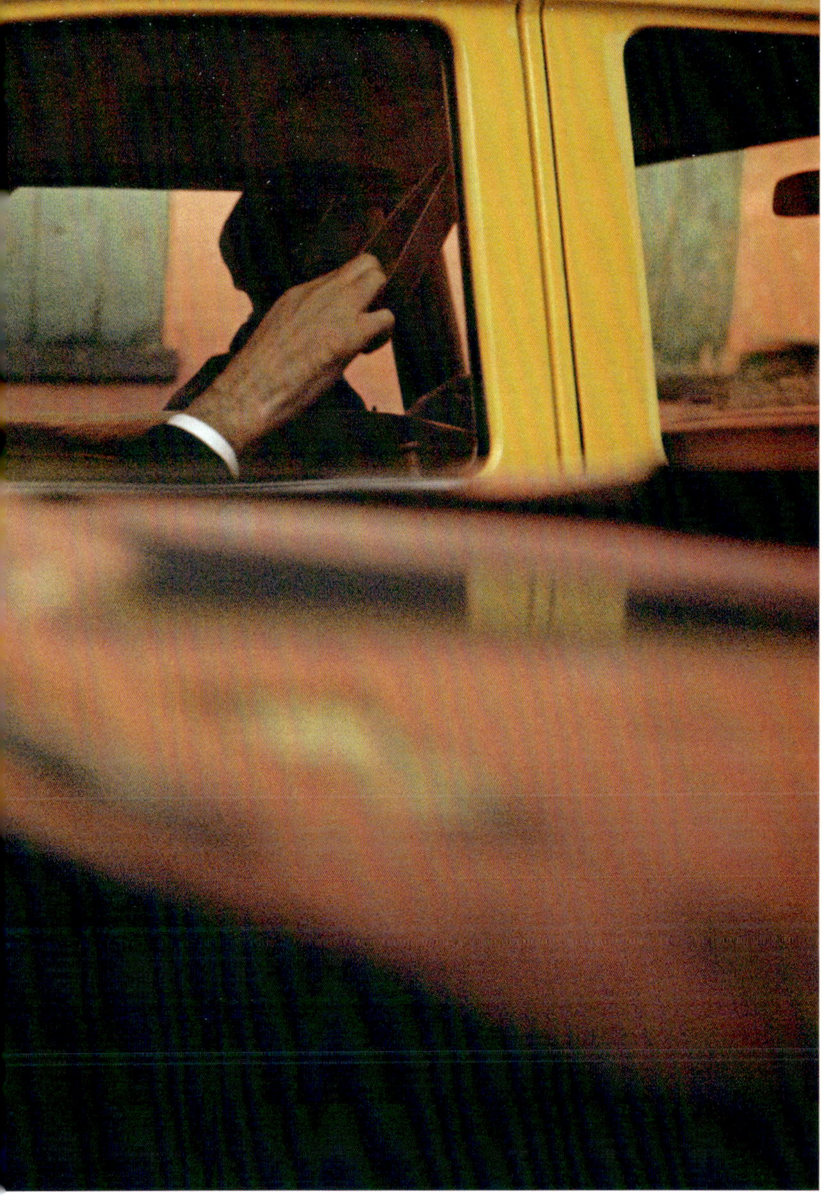

28. Don’t Walk, c. 1952.

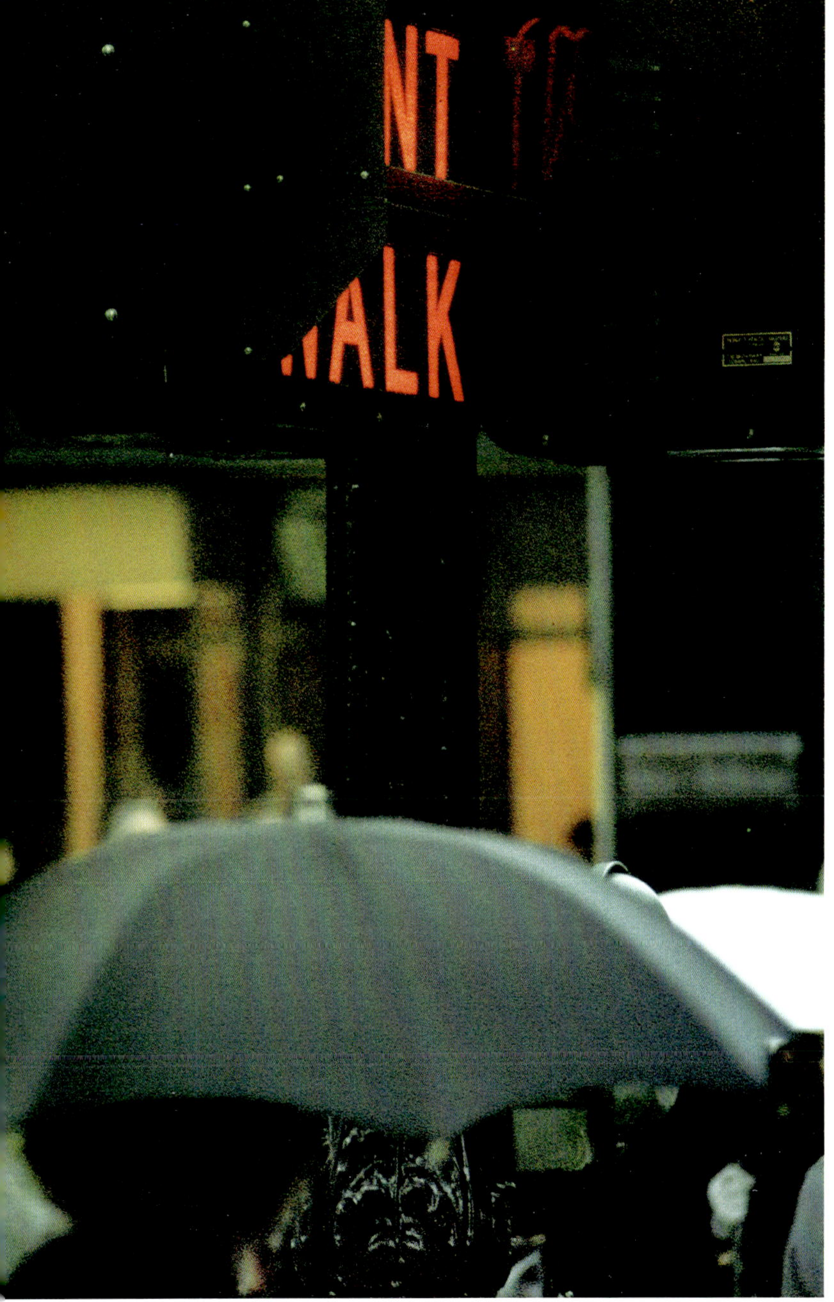
NT
ALK

29. Chauffeur, c. 1955.

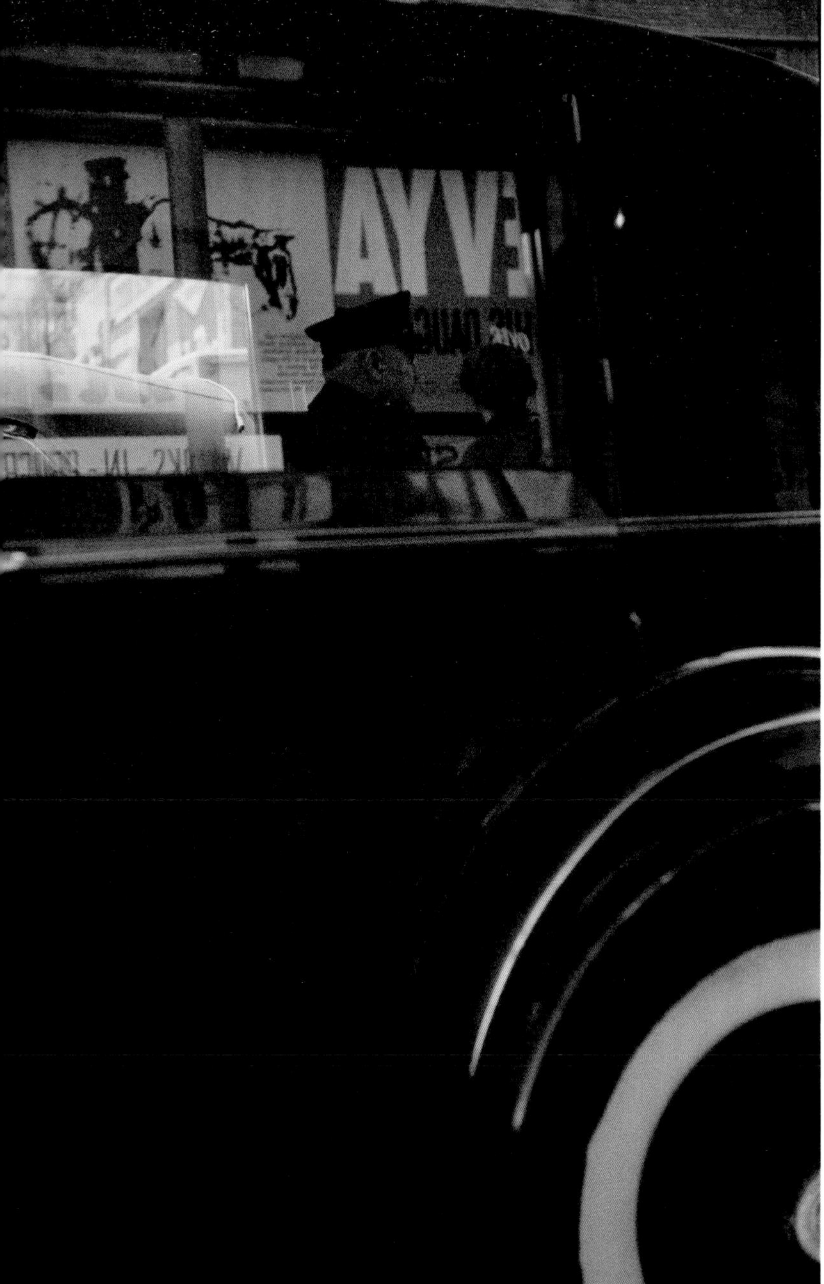

30. Through boards, c. 1957.

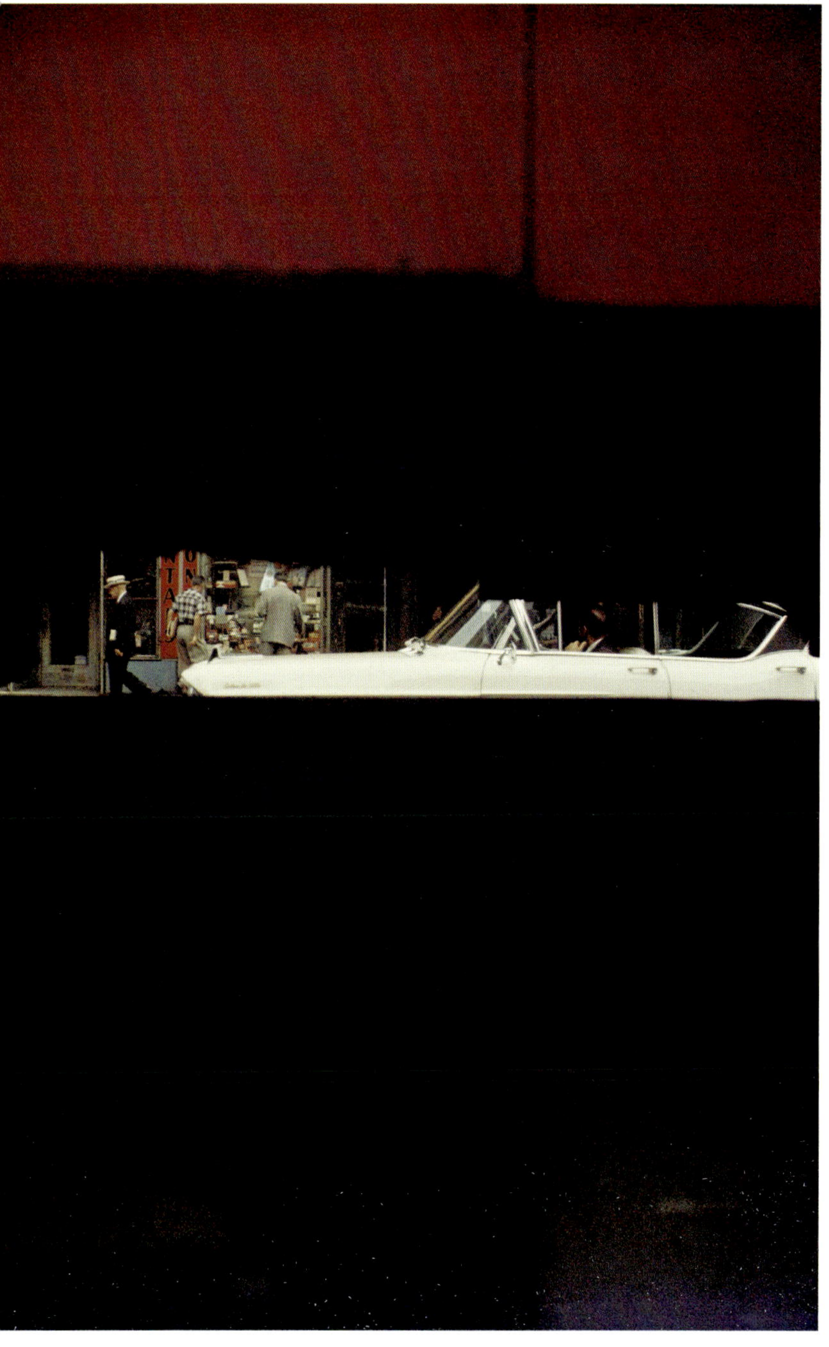

31. El exit, c. 1952.

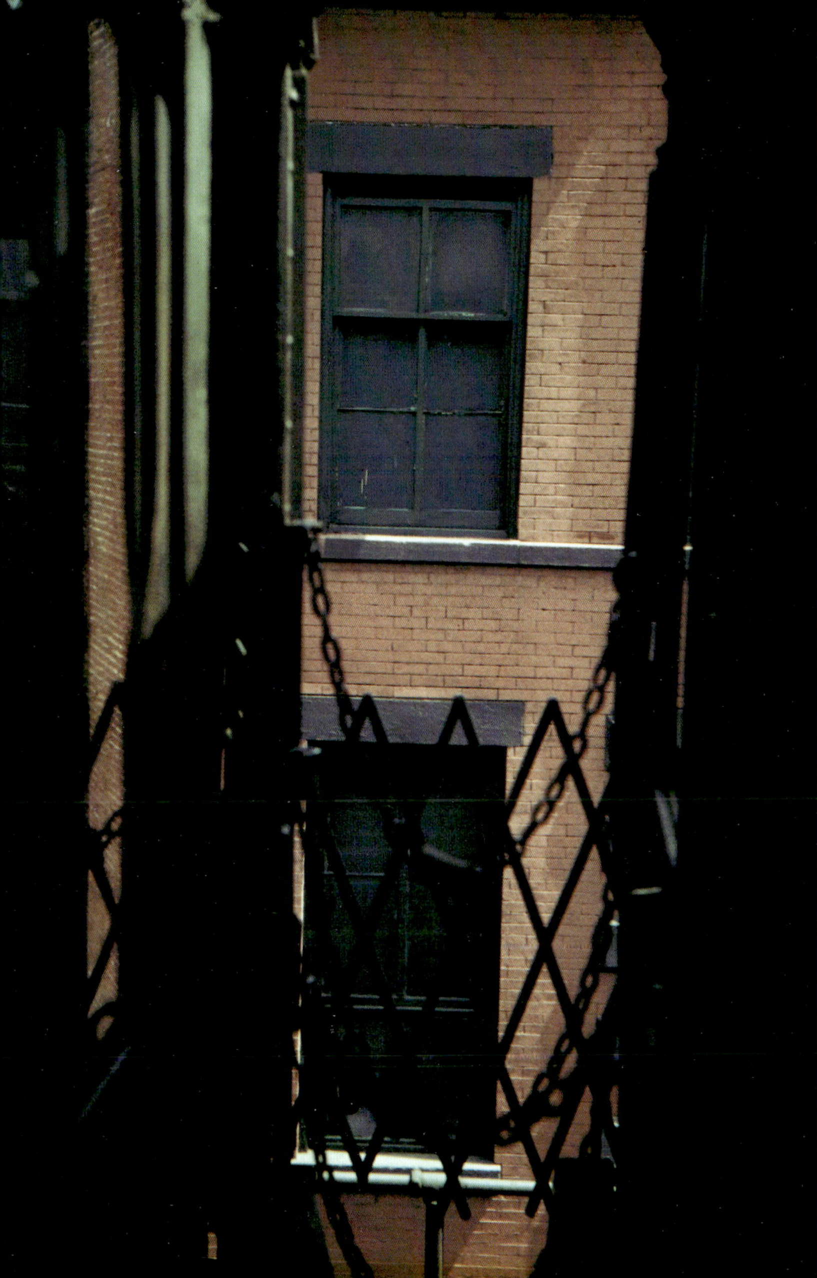

32. Pizza, Paterson, c. 1952.

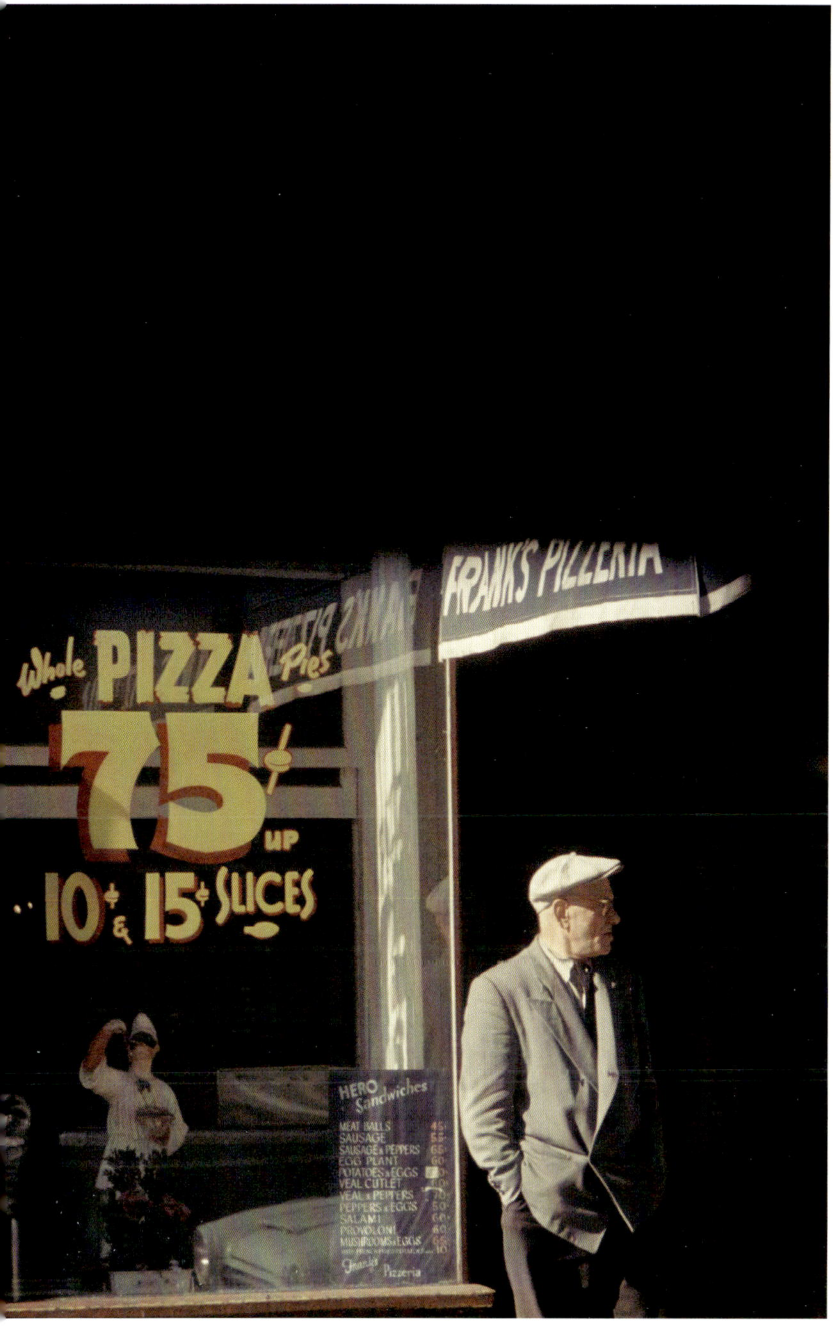

FRANK'S PIZZERIA
Whole PIZZA Pies
75¢ up
10¢ & 15¢ SLICES
HERO Sandwiches
MEAT BALLS
SAUSAGE
SAUSAGE & PEPPERS
EGG PLANT
POTATOES & EGGS
VEAL CUTLET
VEAL & PEPPERS
PEPPERS & EGGS
SALAMI
PROVOLONI
MUSHROOMS & EGGS
Frank's Pizzeria

33. Street scene, c. 1959.

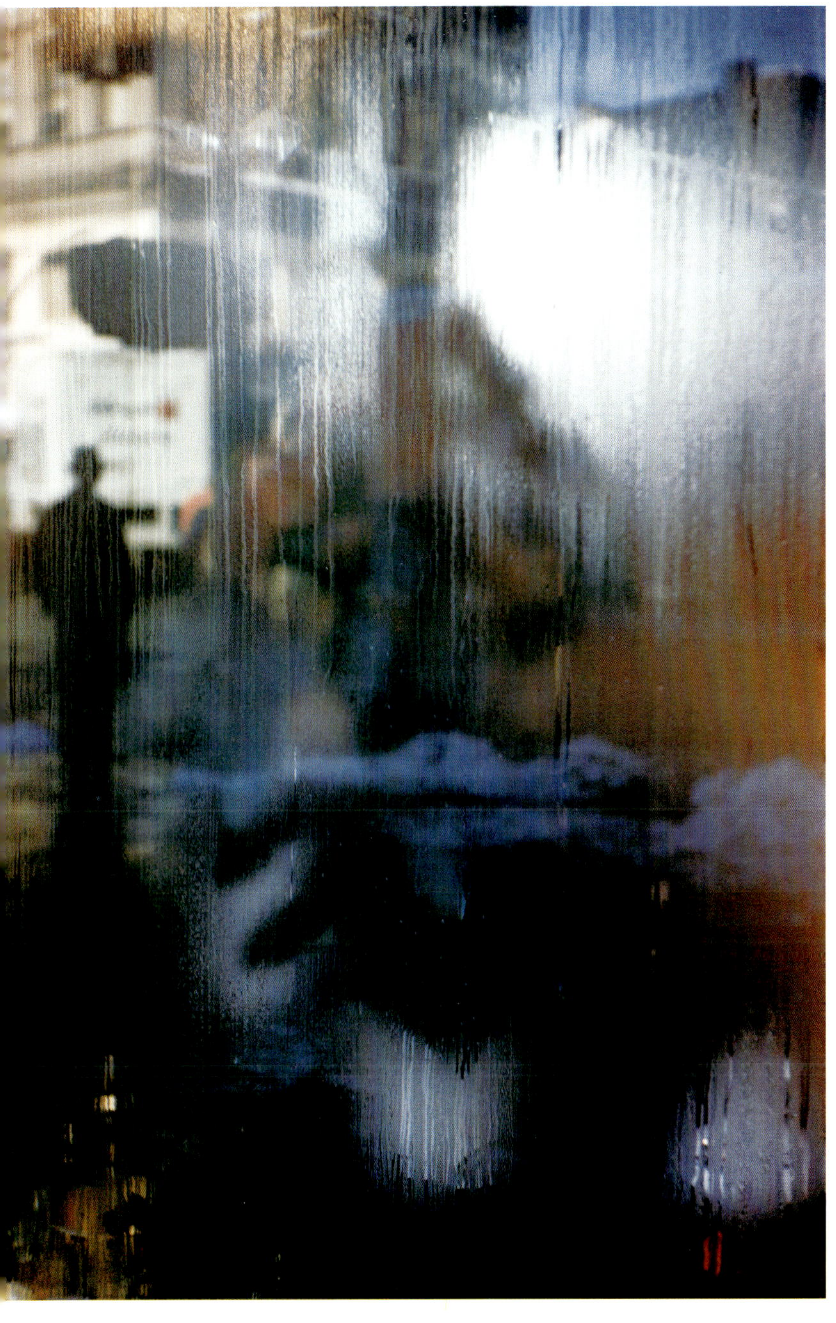

34. Mannequin, c. 1952.

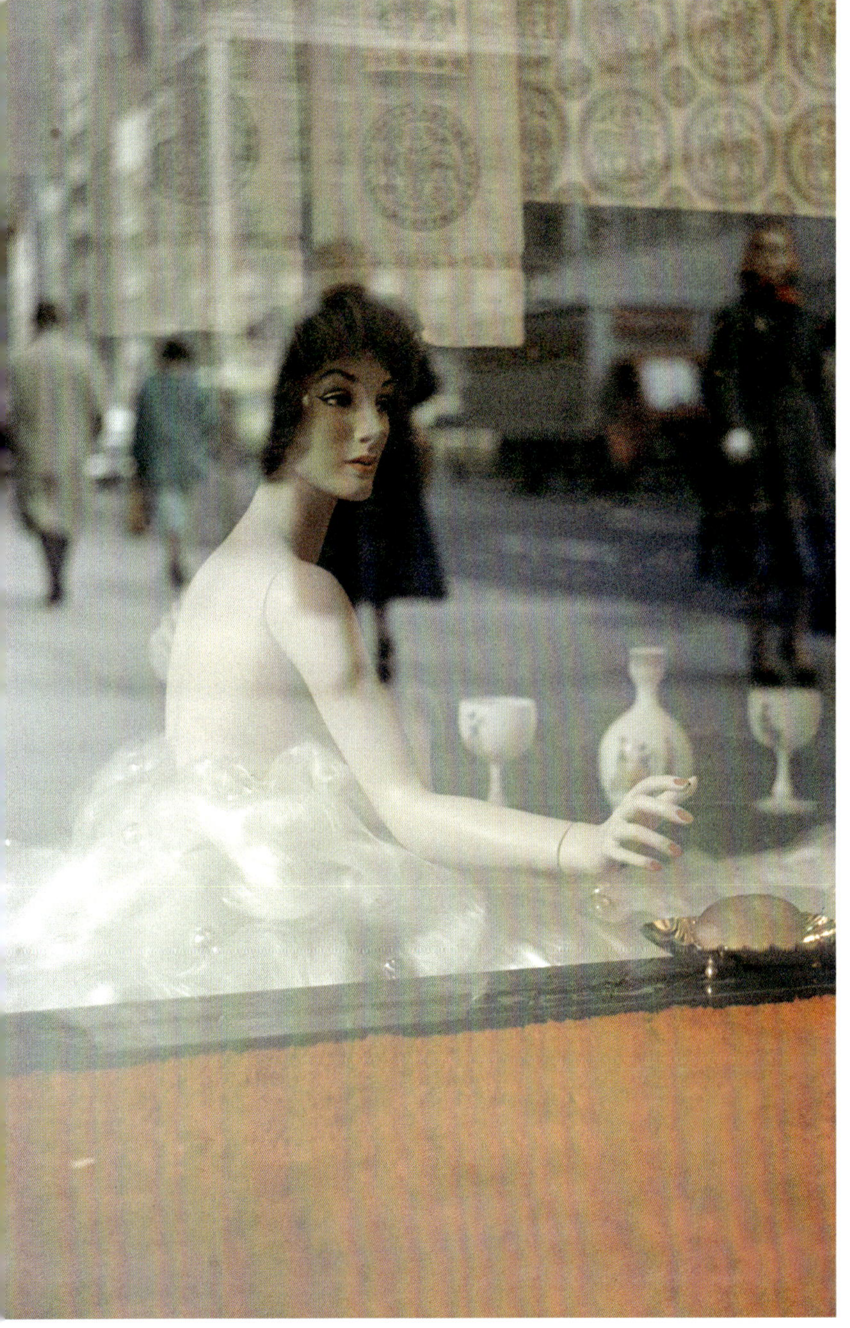

35. Barbara hides, c. 1945.

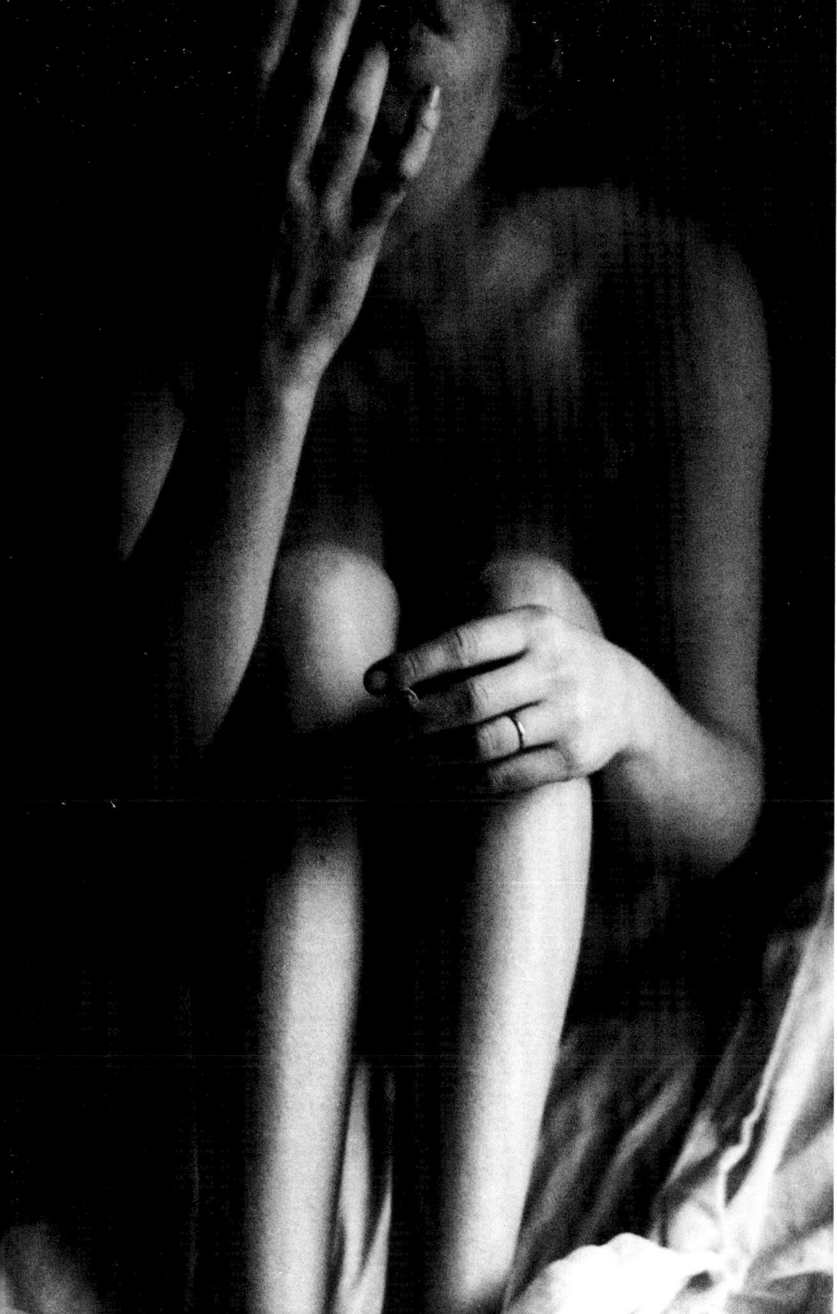

36. Sleep, c. 1955.

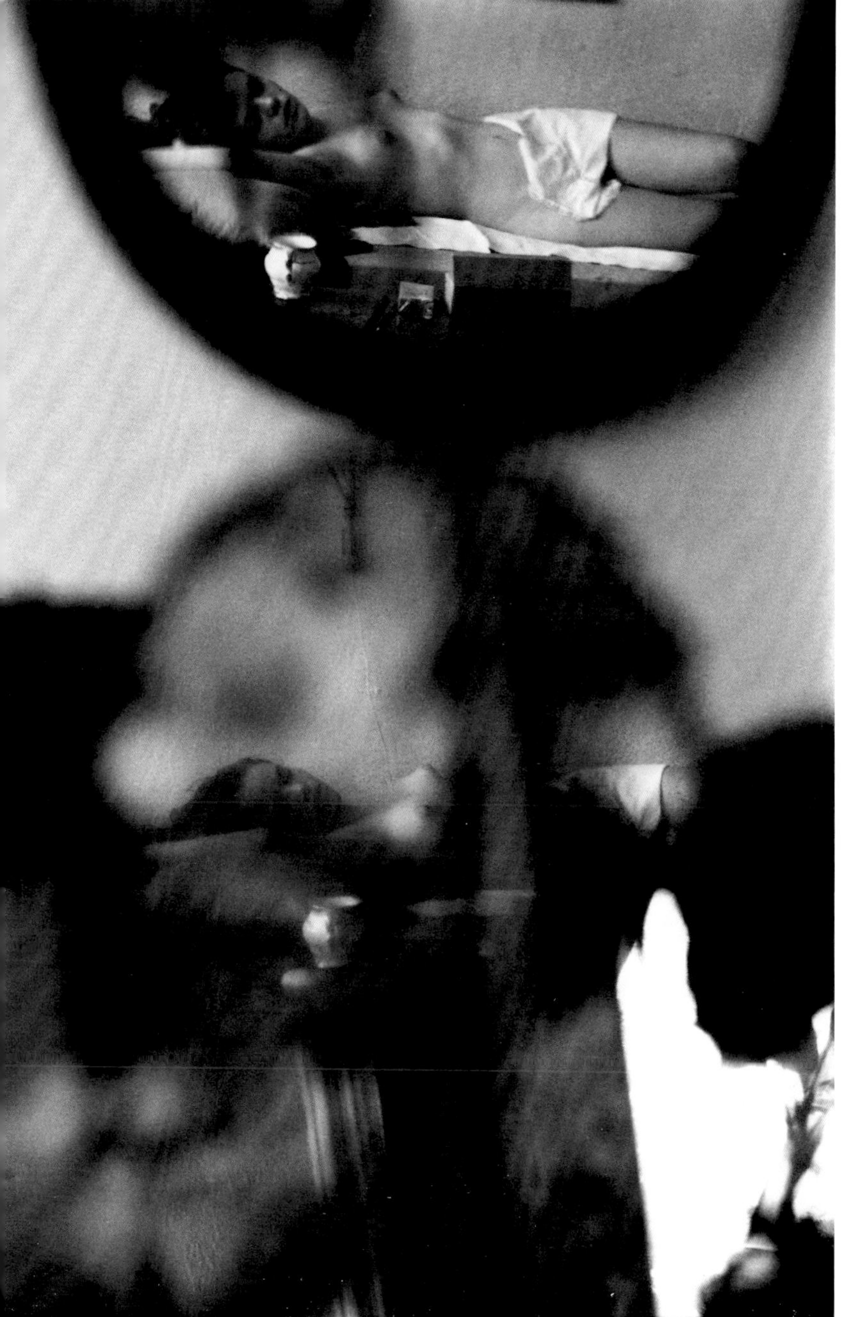

37. Halloween, c. 1952.

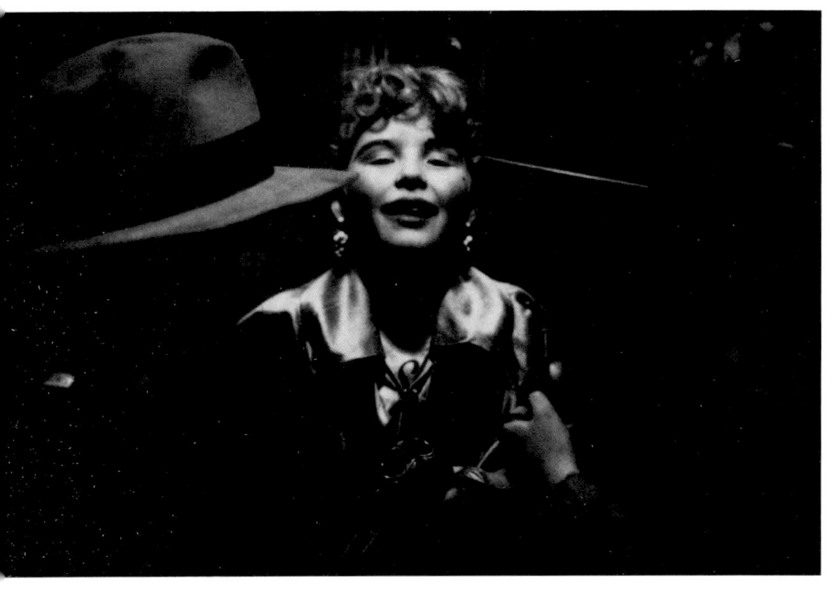

38. *Harper's Bazaar*, c. 1960.

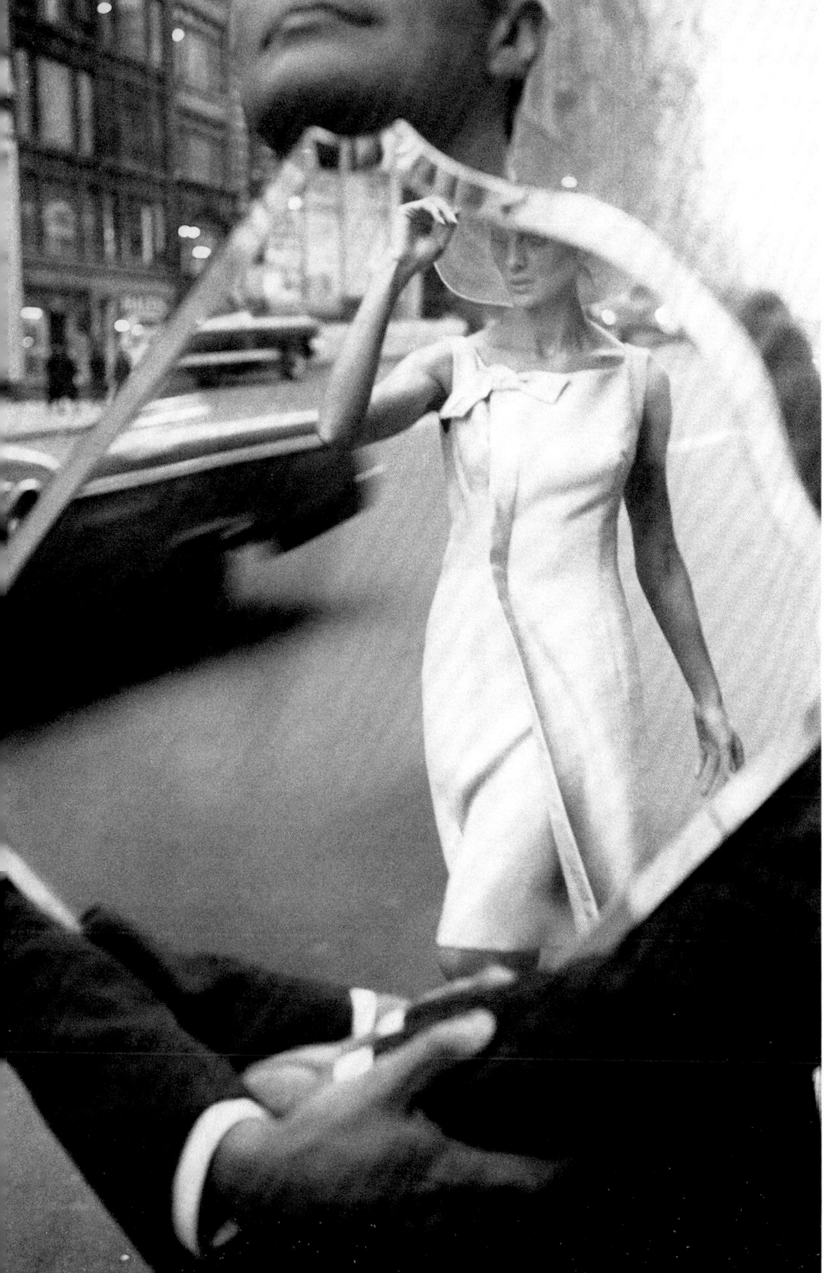

39. Shopping, c. 1953.

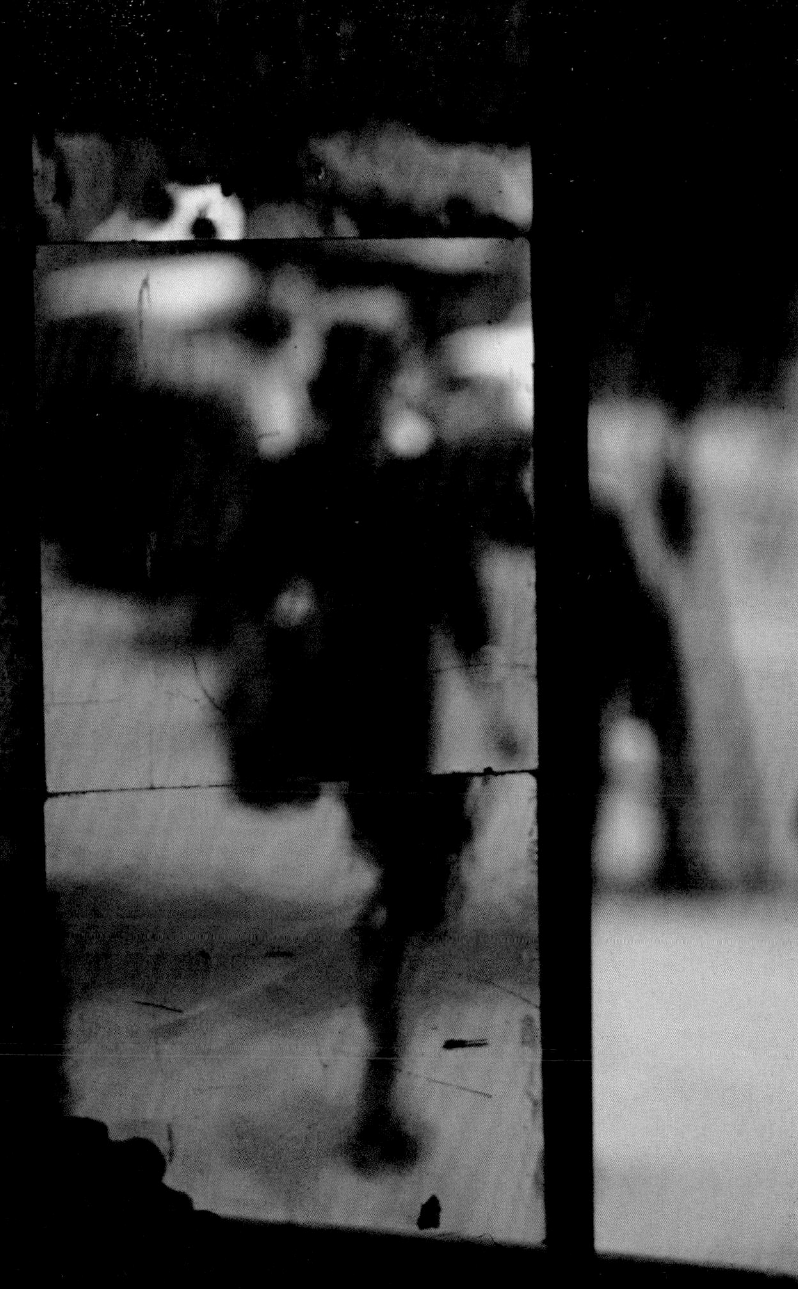

40. Party, c. 1953.

Overleaf:

41. Barbara, c. 1951.

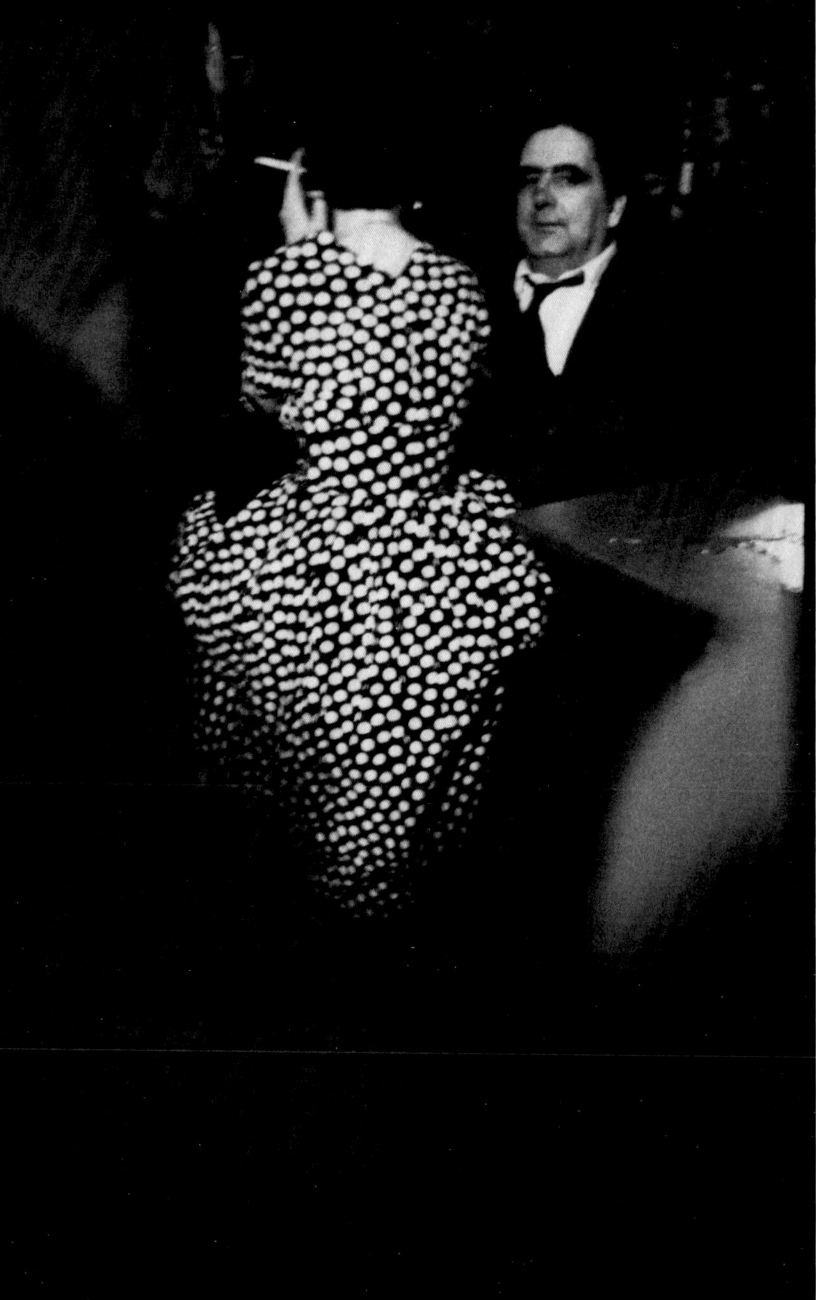

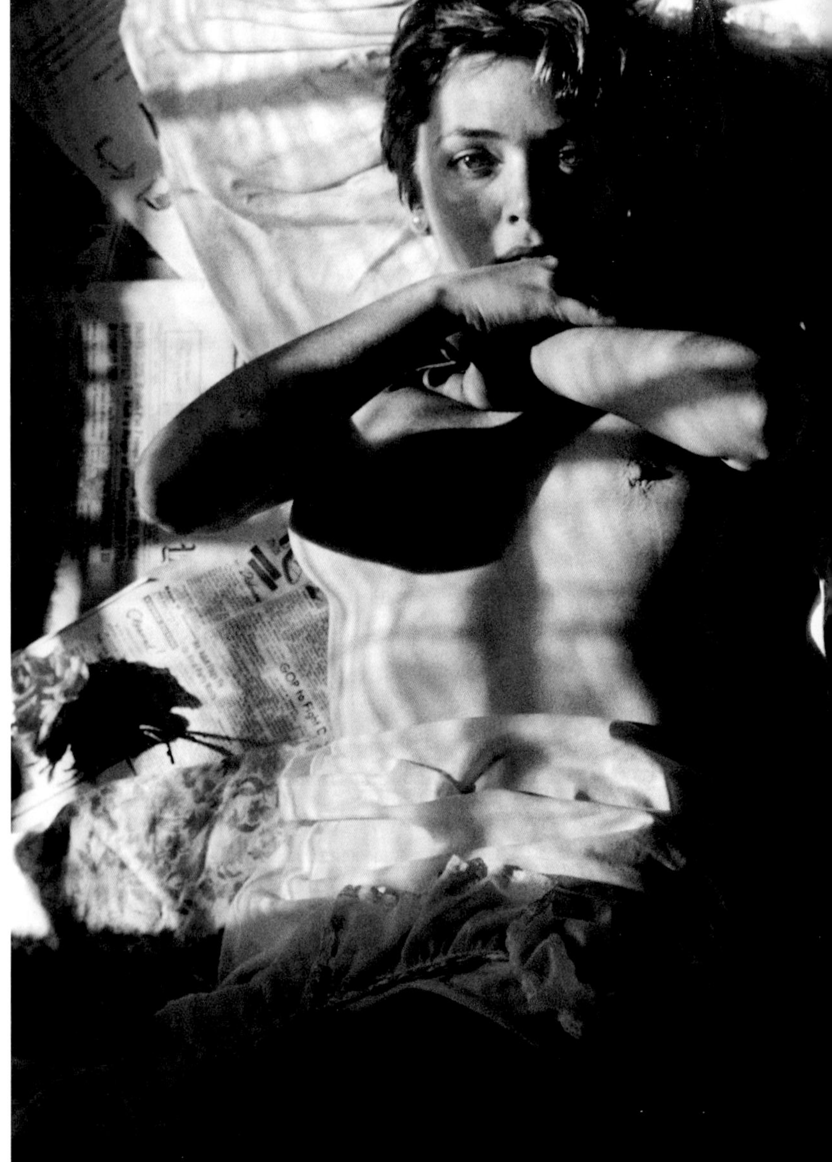
GOP to Fight

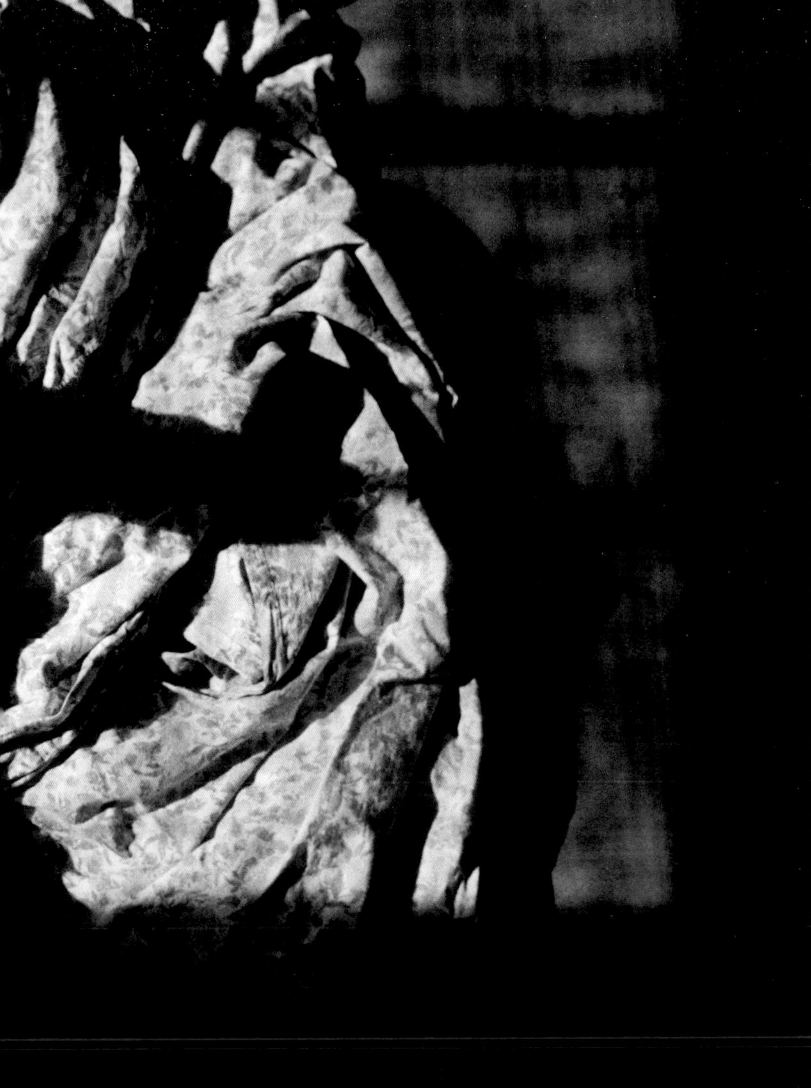

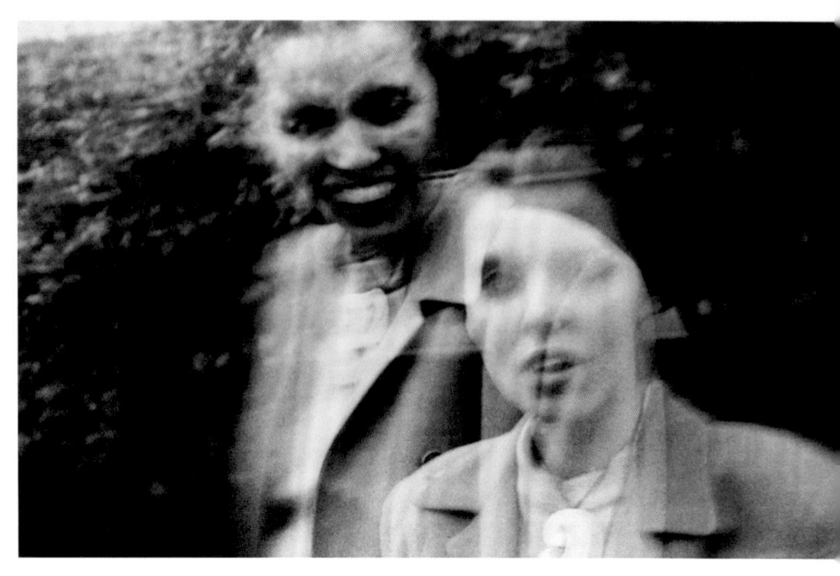

42. Evelyn Pousette-Dart, c. 1947.

43. Jean Pearson, c. 1948.

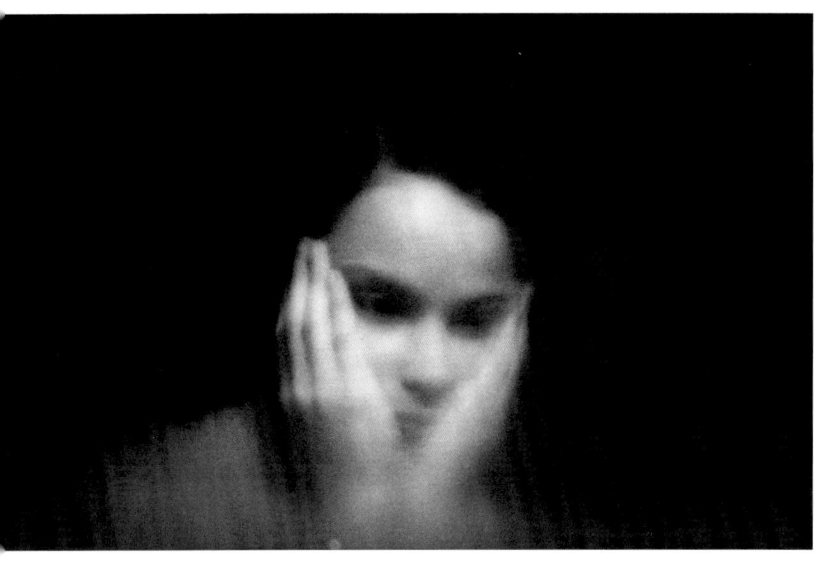

44. Plum umbrella, c. 1957.

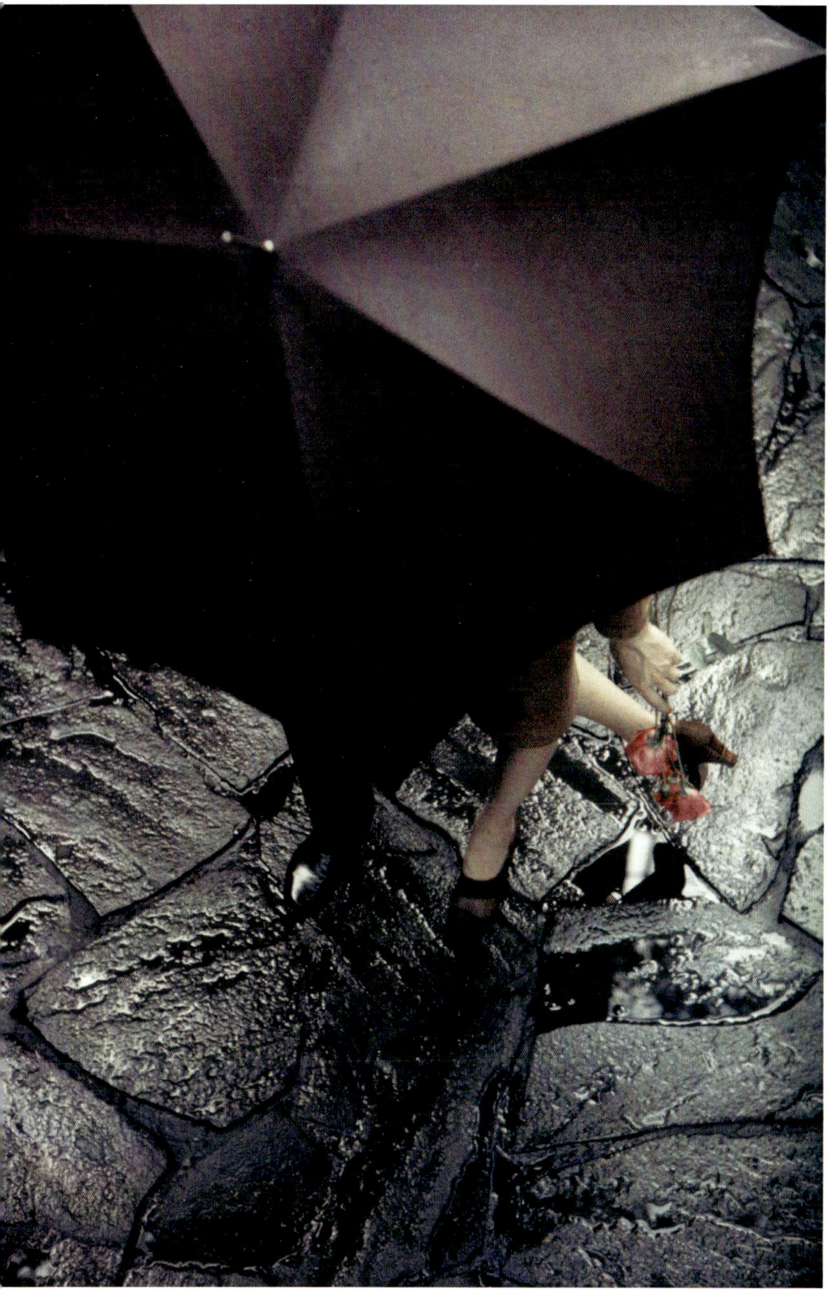

45. Baseball, 1953.

46. Untitled, 1961.

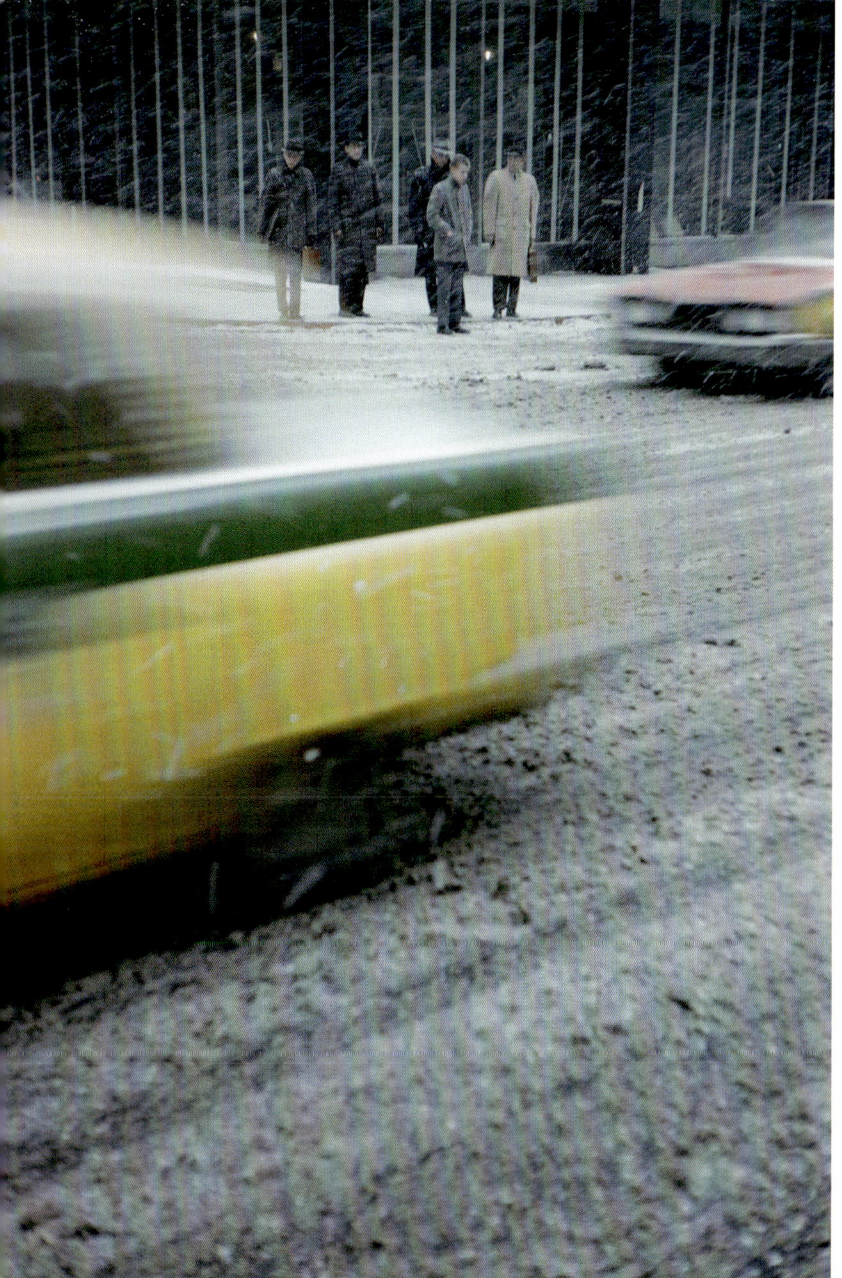

47. Seamstress, c. 1952.

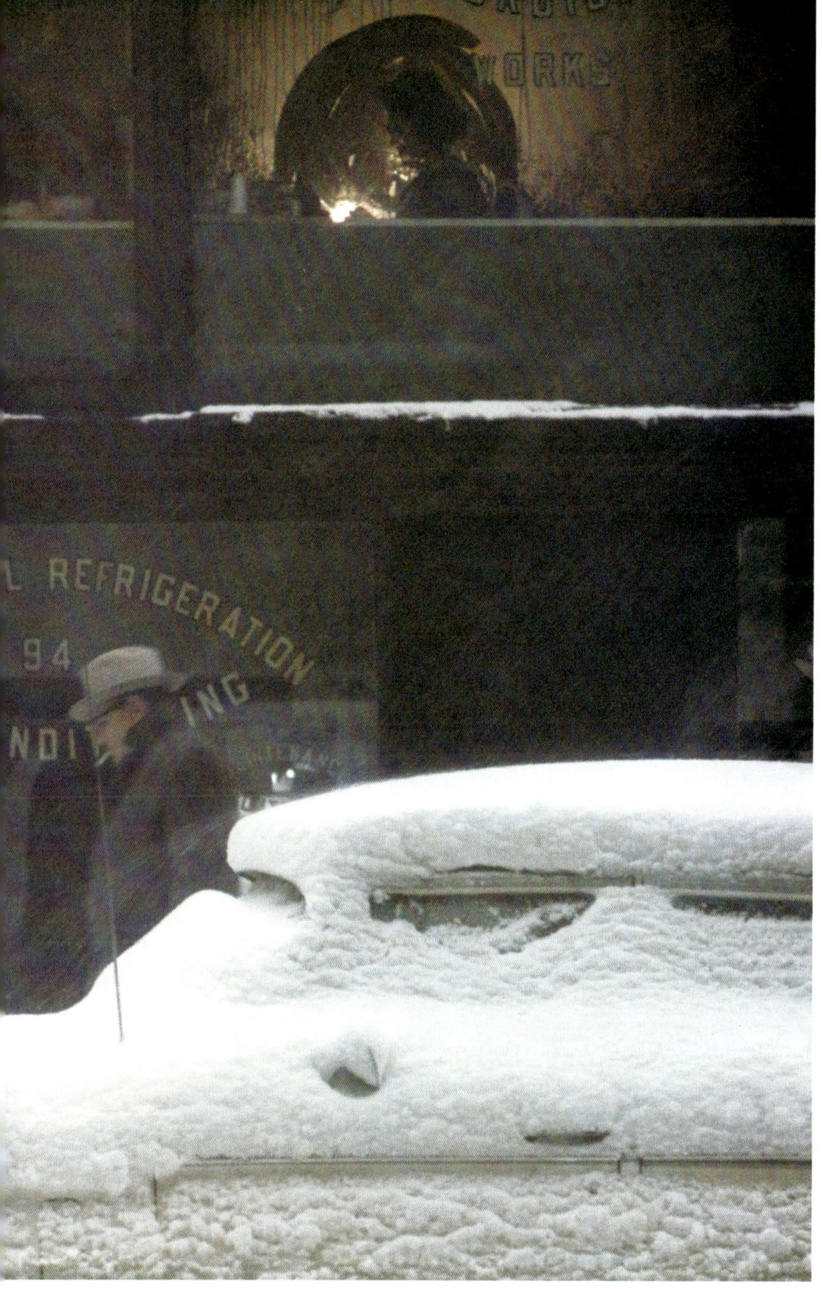
WORKS
L REFRIGERATION
94
ING
NDI

48. Untitled, undated.

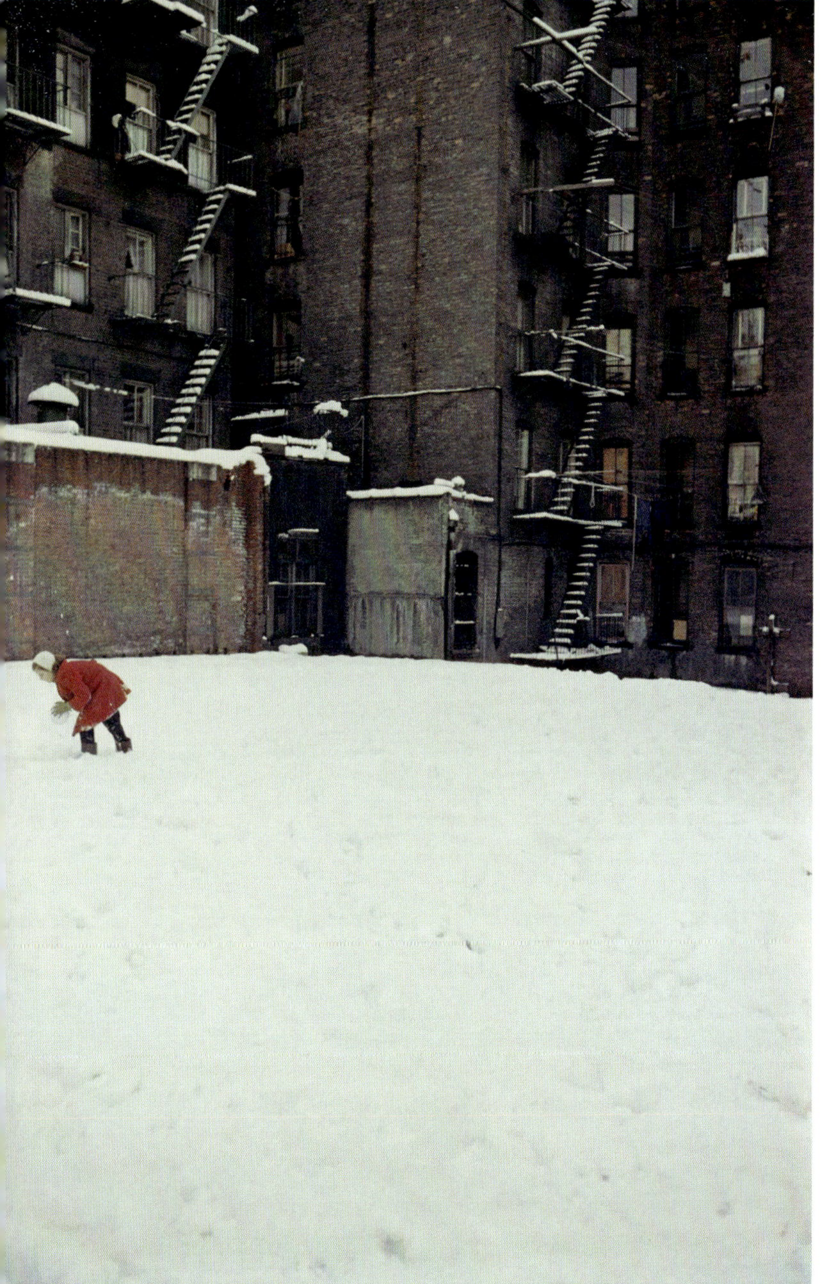

49. Smoker, c. 1963.

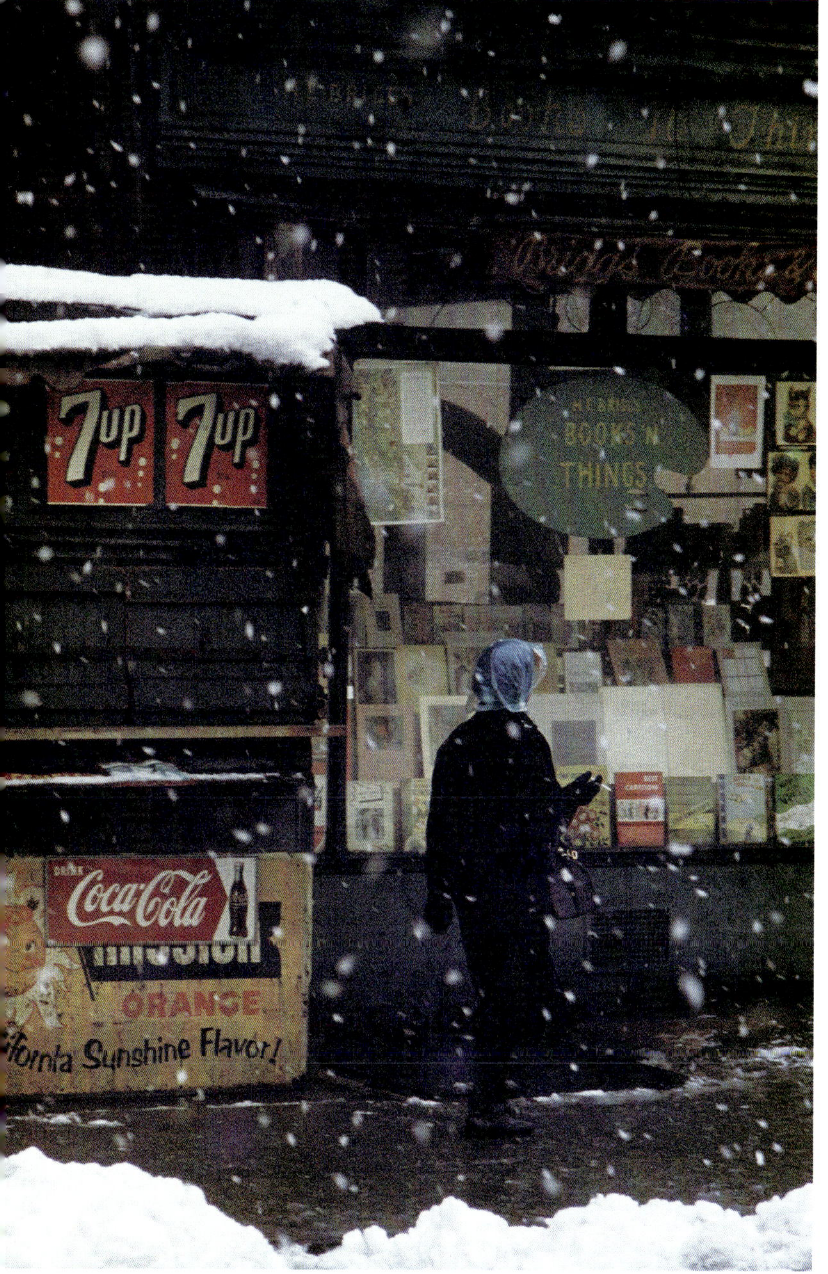

7up
7up
BOOKS 'N' THINGS
Coca-Cola
ORANGE
Sunshine Flavor!

50. Red umbrella, c. 1963.

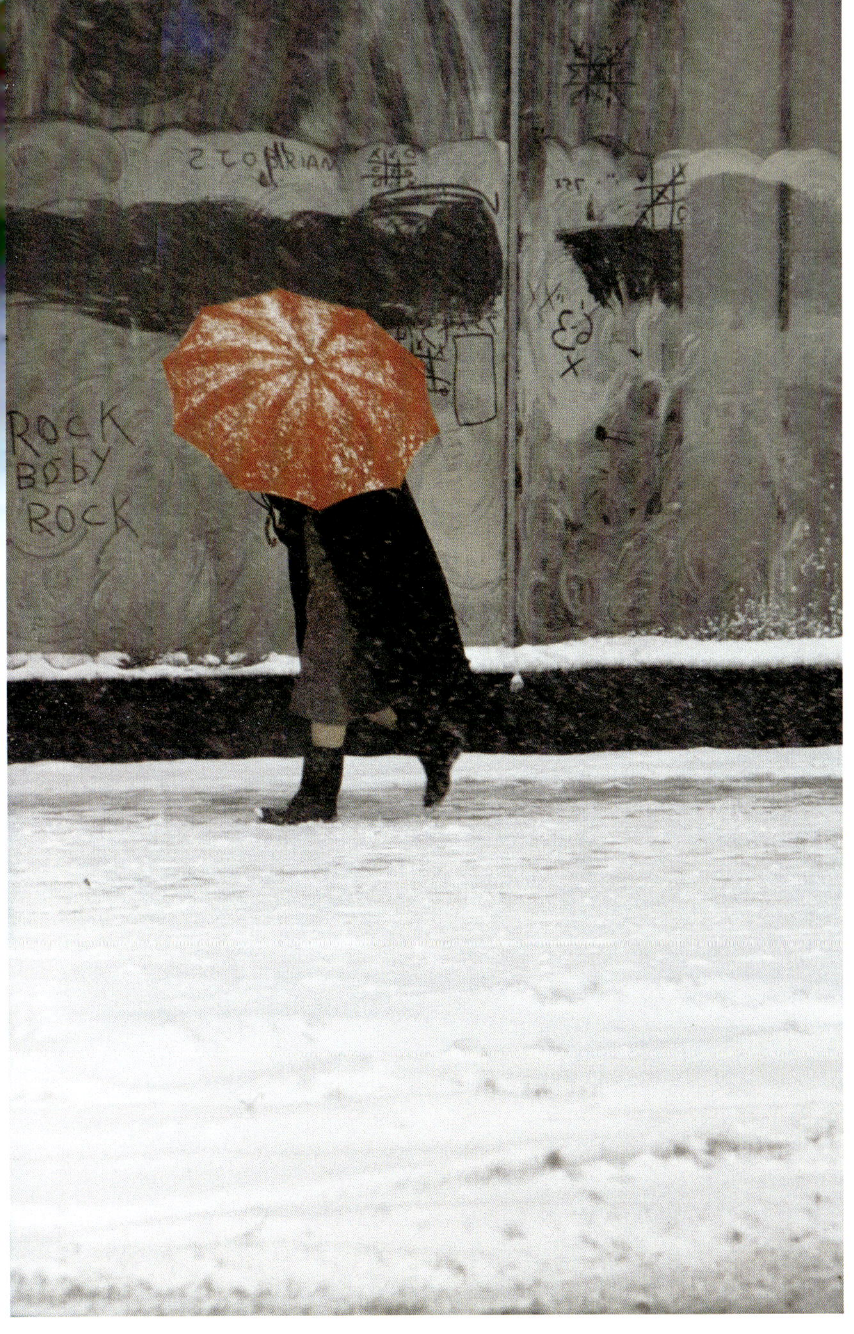
ROCK
BABY
ROCK

51. Red light, c. 1957.

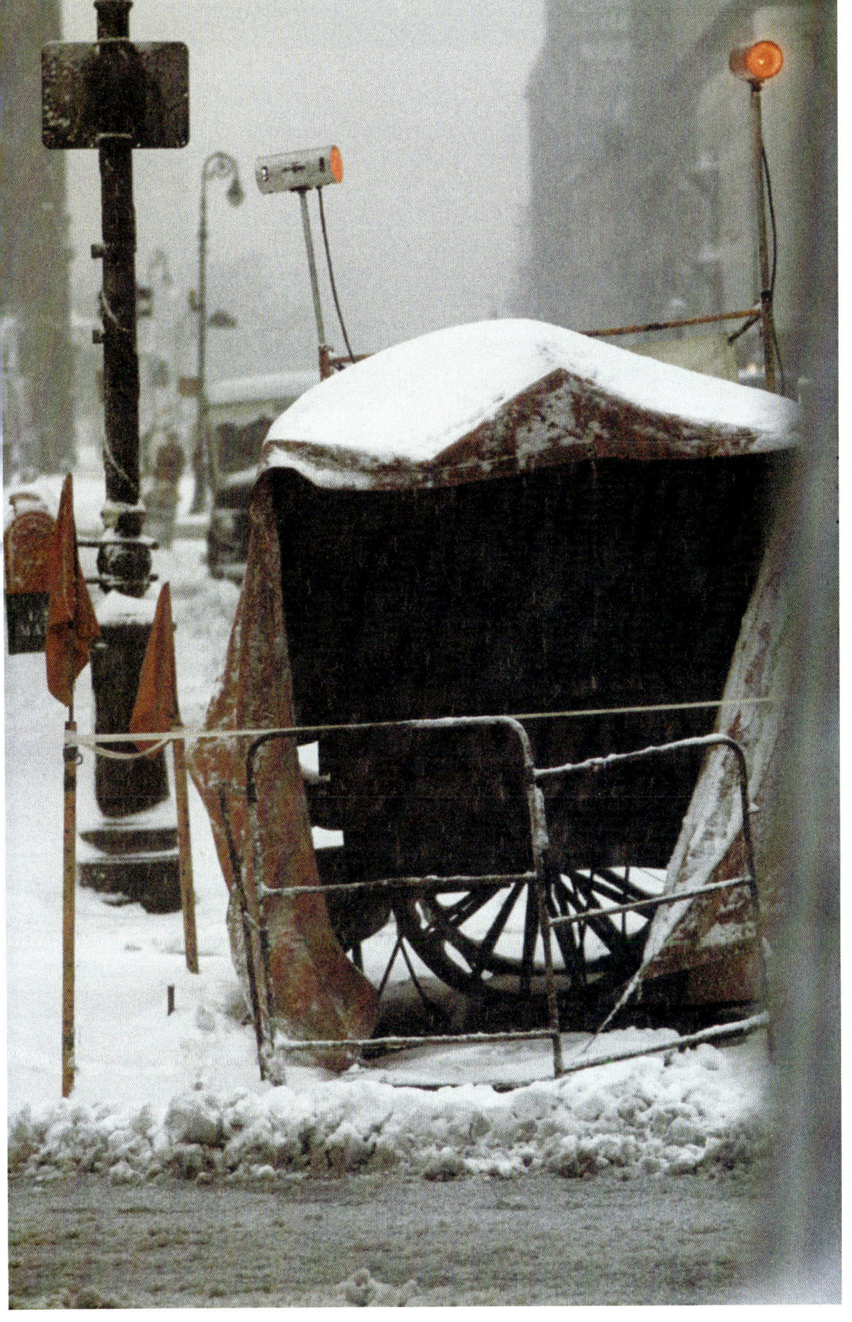

52. Chinatown, c. 1956.

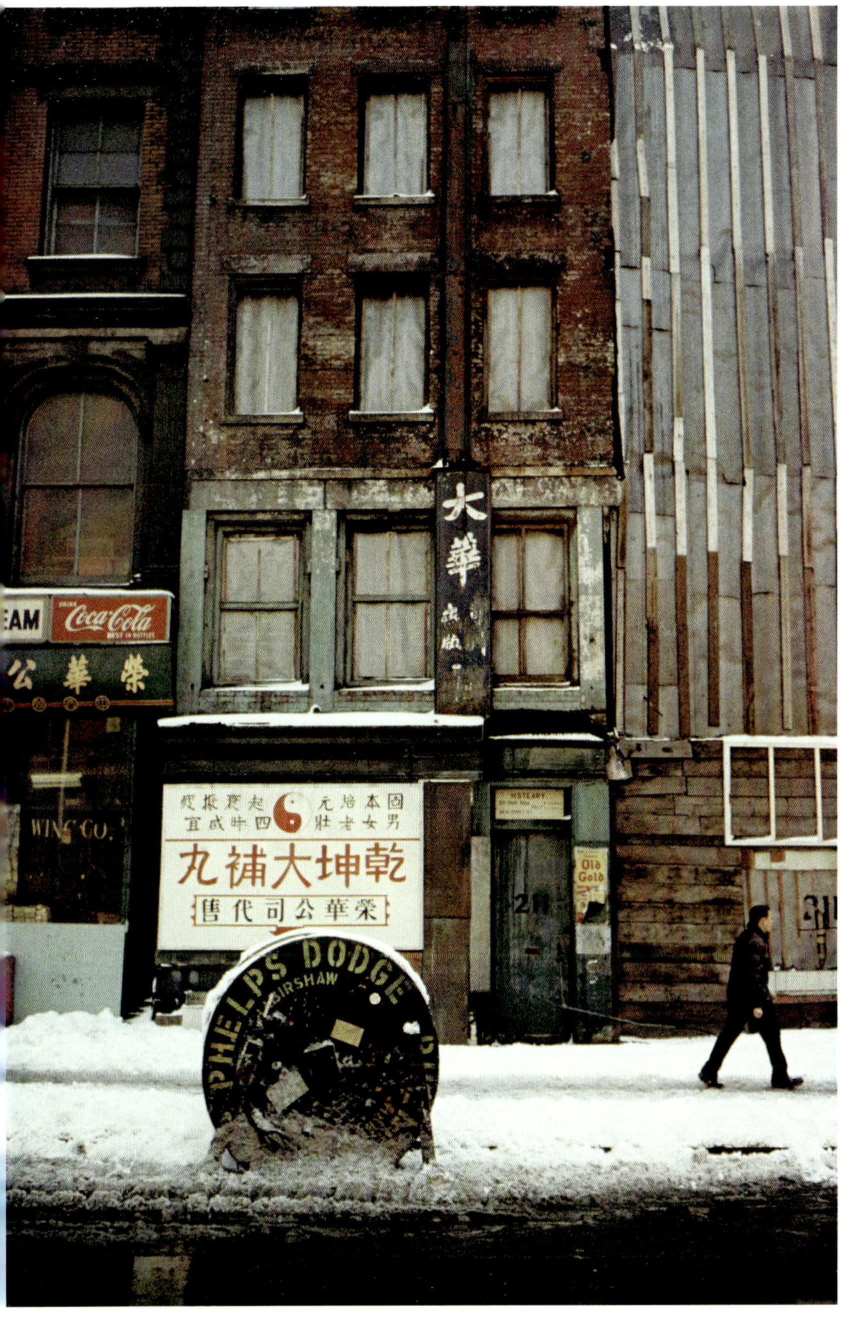
EAM
Coca-Cola
榮華公
大華
WING CO.
乾坤大補丸
榮華公司代售
Old Gold
PHELPS DODGE
BIRSHAW

53. Worker, c. 1956.

Overleaf:

54. El, c. 1954.

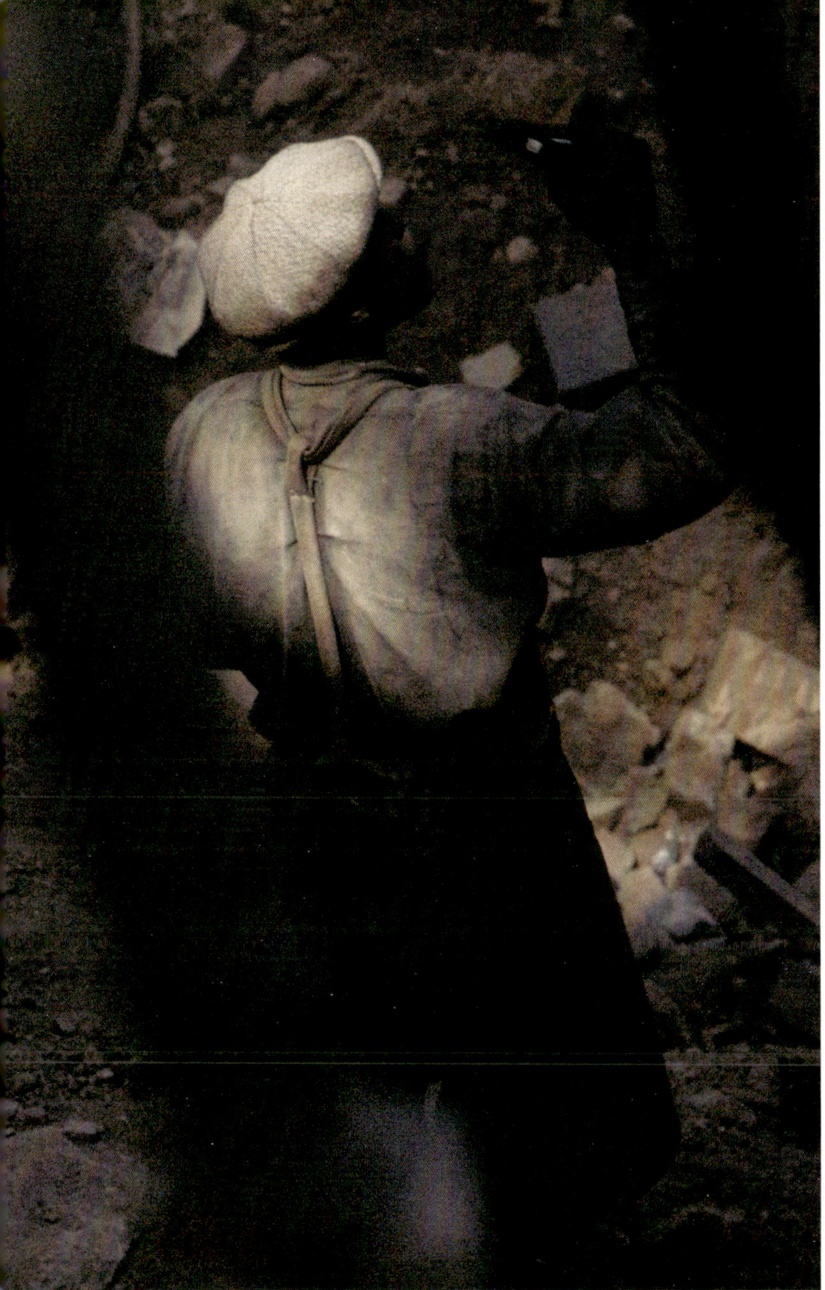

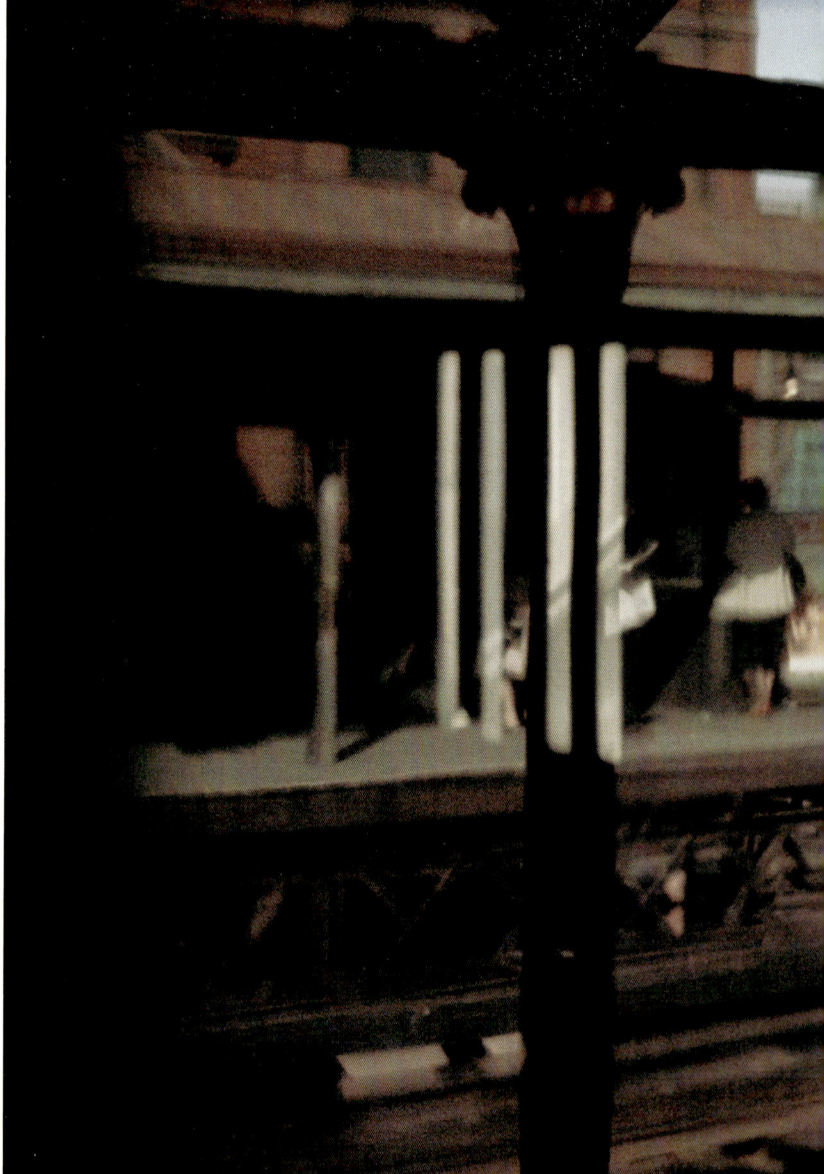

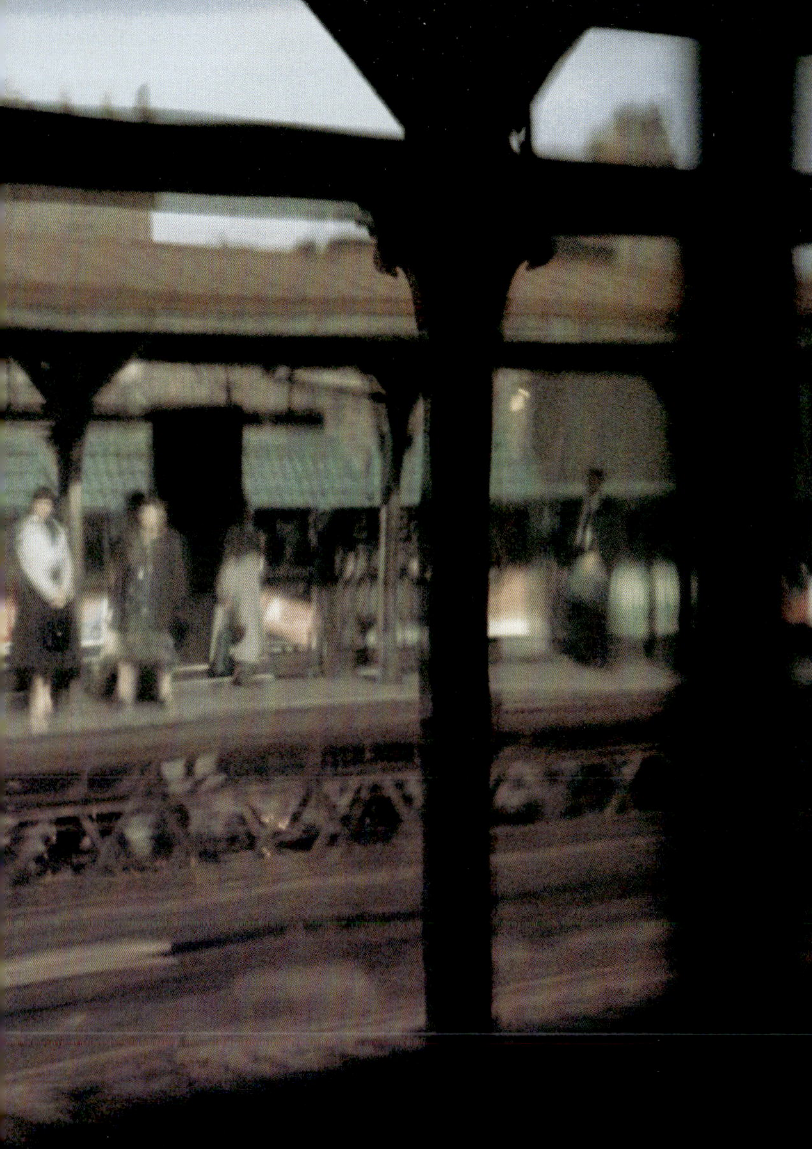

55. Tanager Stairs, c. 1954.

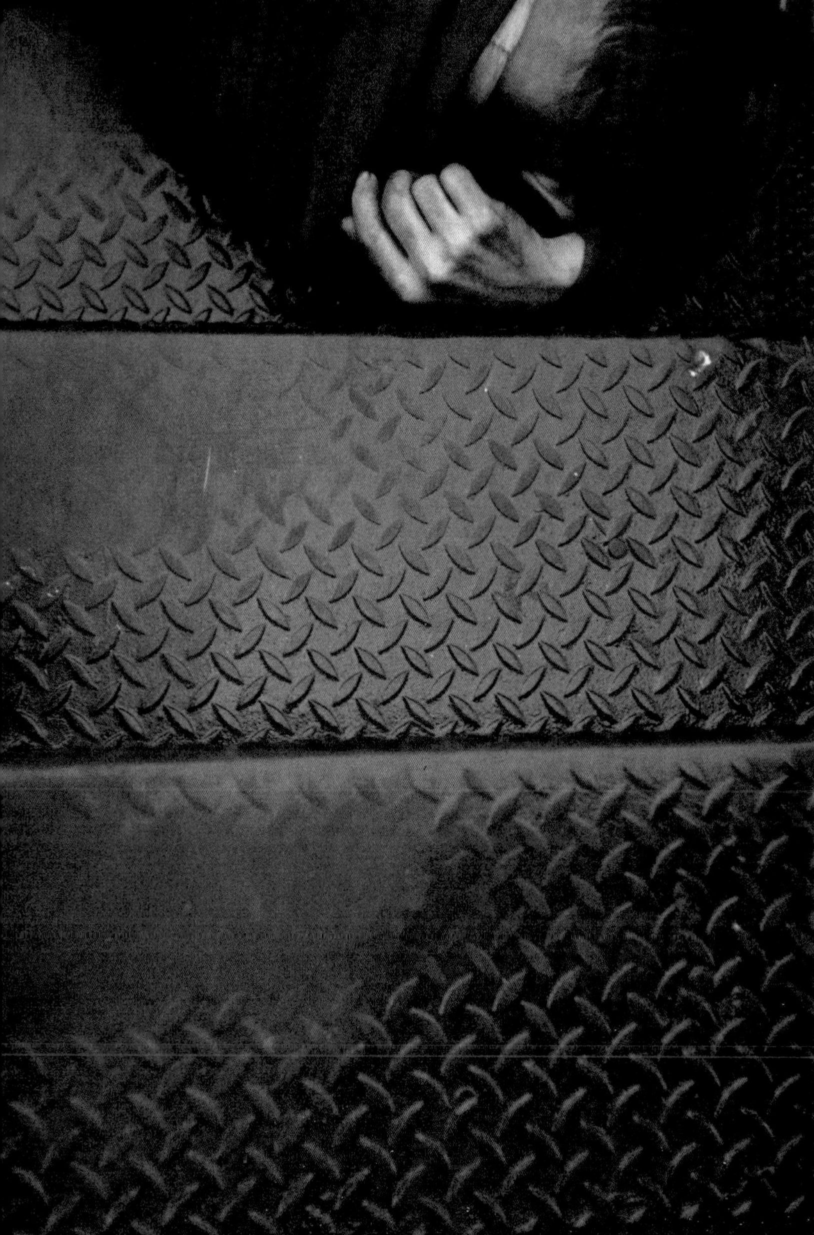

56. Foot on El, c. 1954.

Overleaf:

57. Horse, c. 1958.

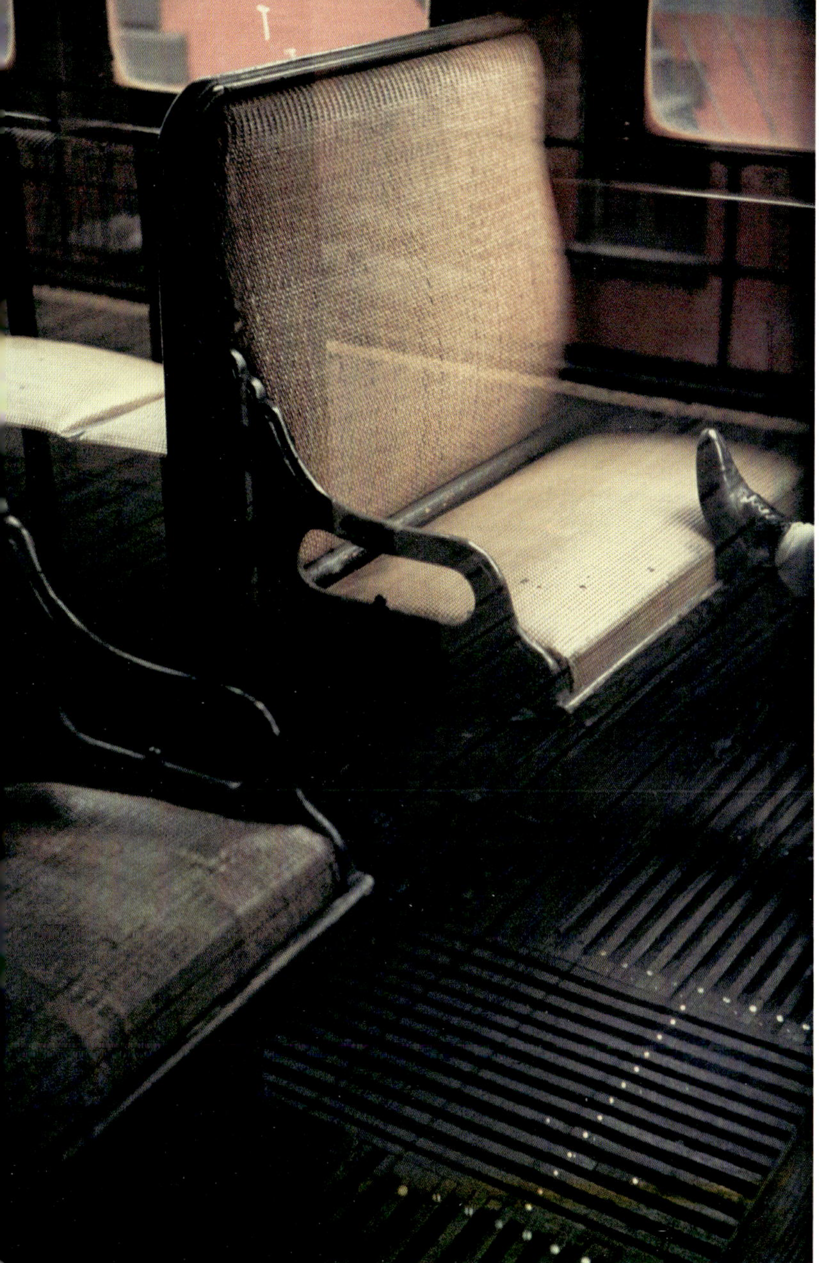

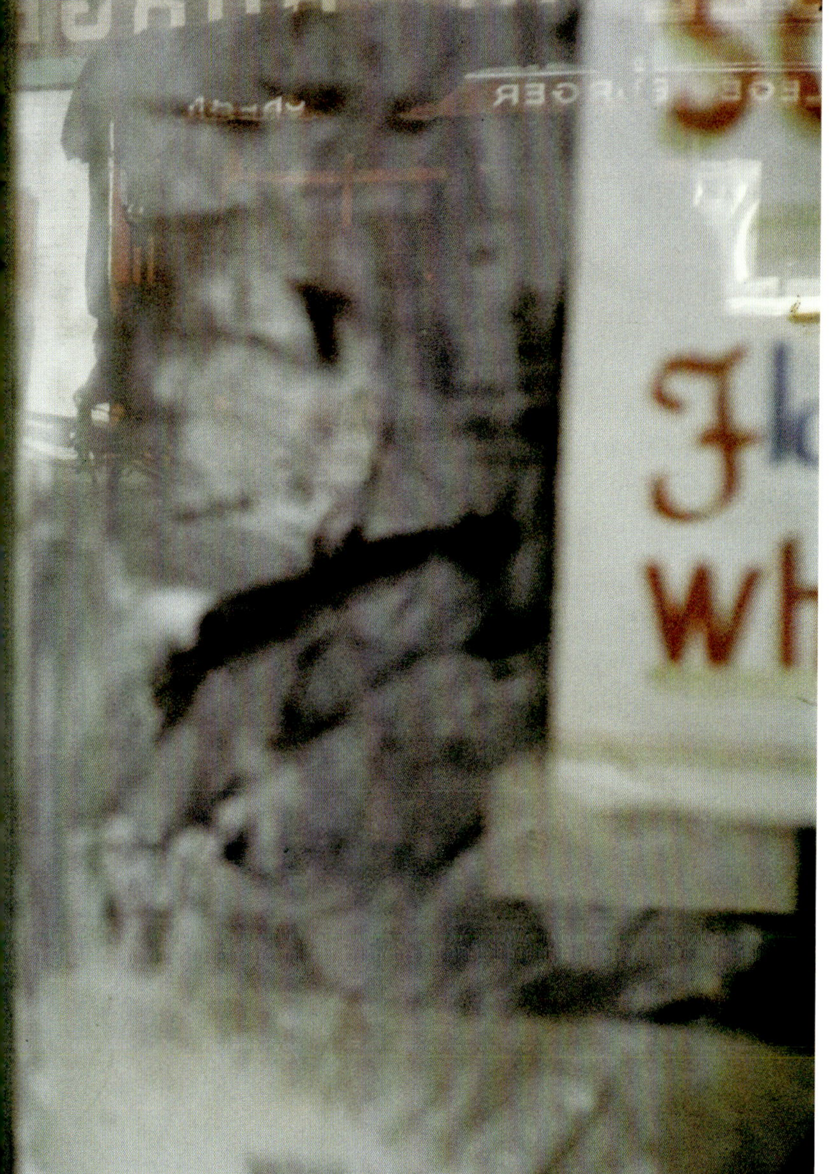

58. Two ladies, c. 1948.

Overleaf:

59. Kathy and Gloria, c. 1947.

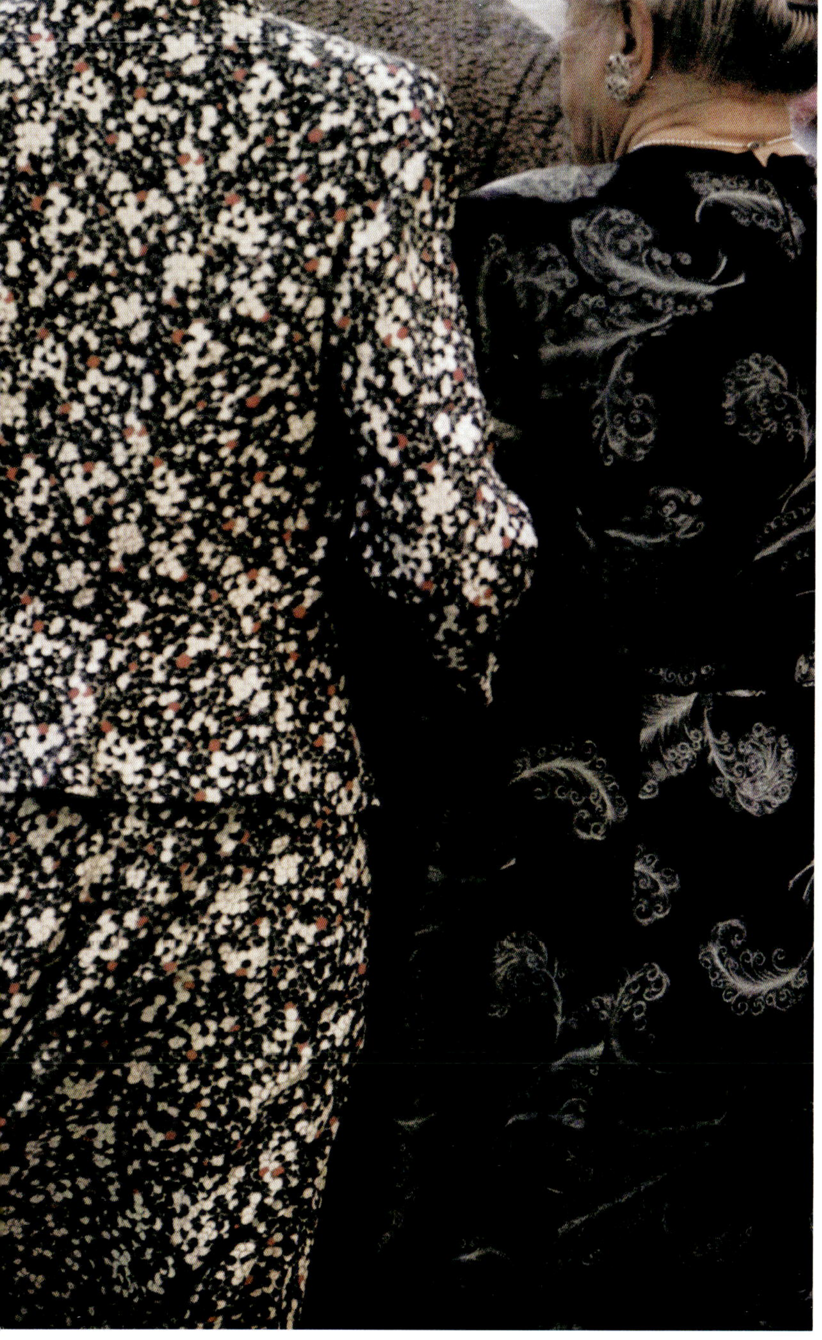

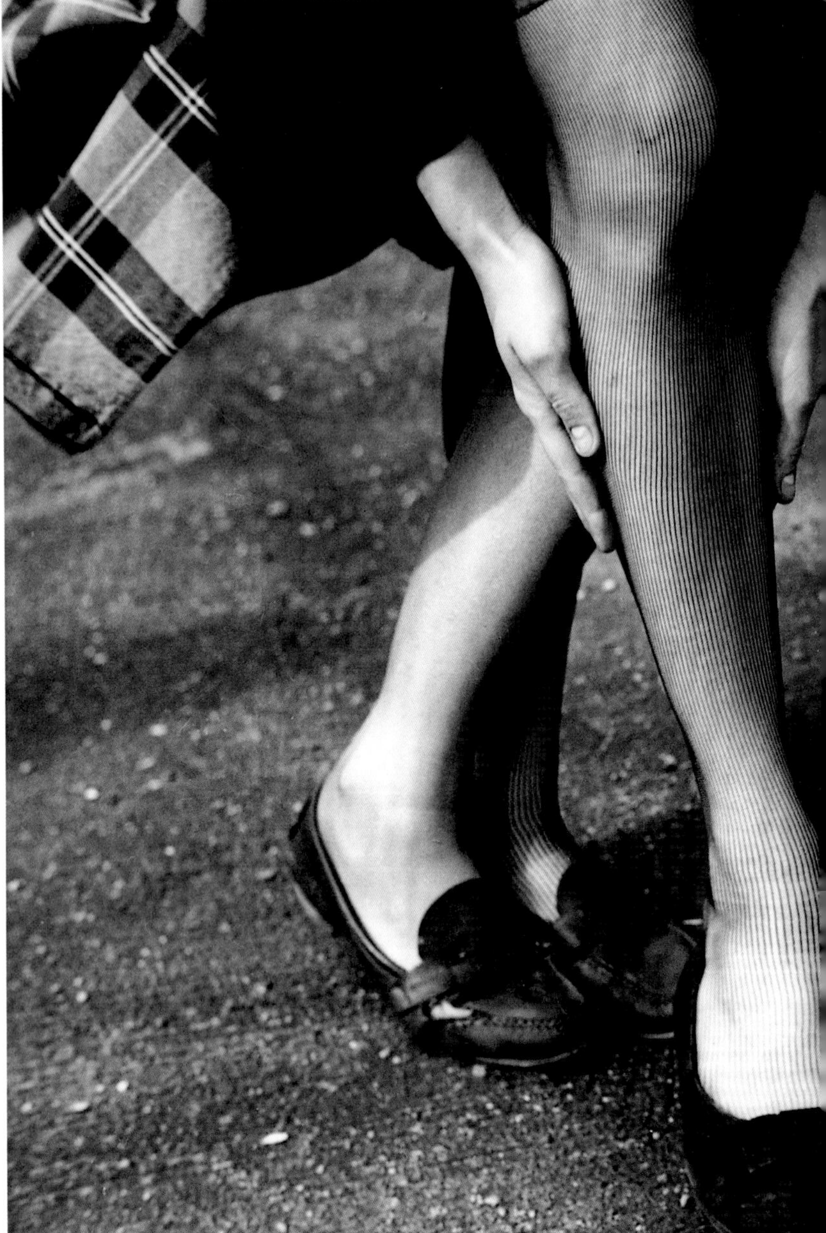

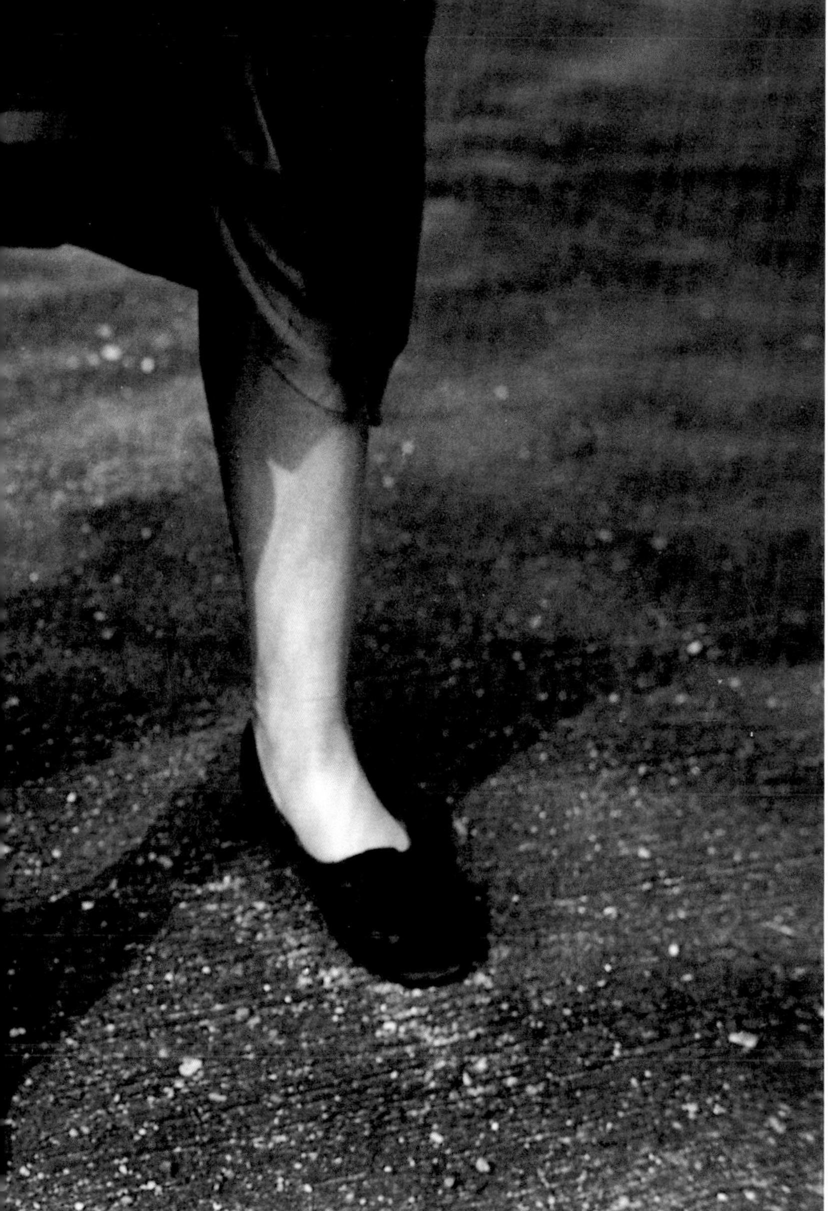

60. Mary Jane Russell (for *Harper's Bazaar*), c. 1960.

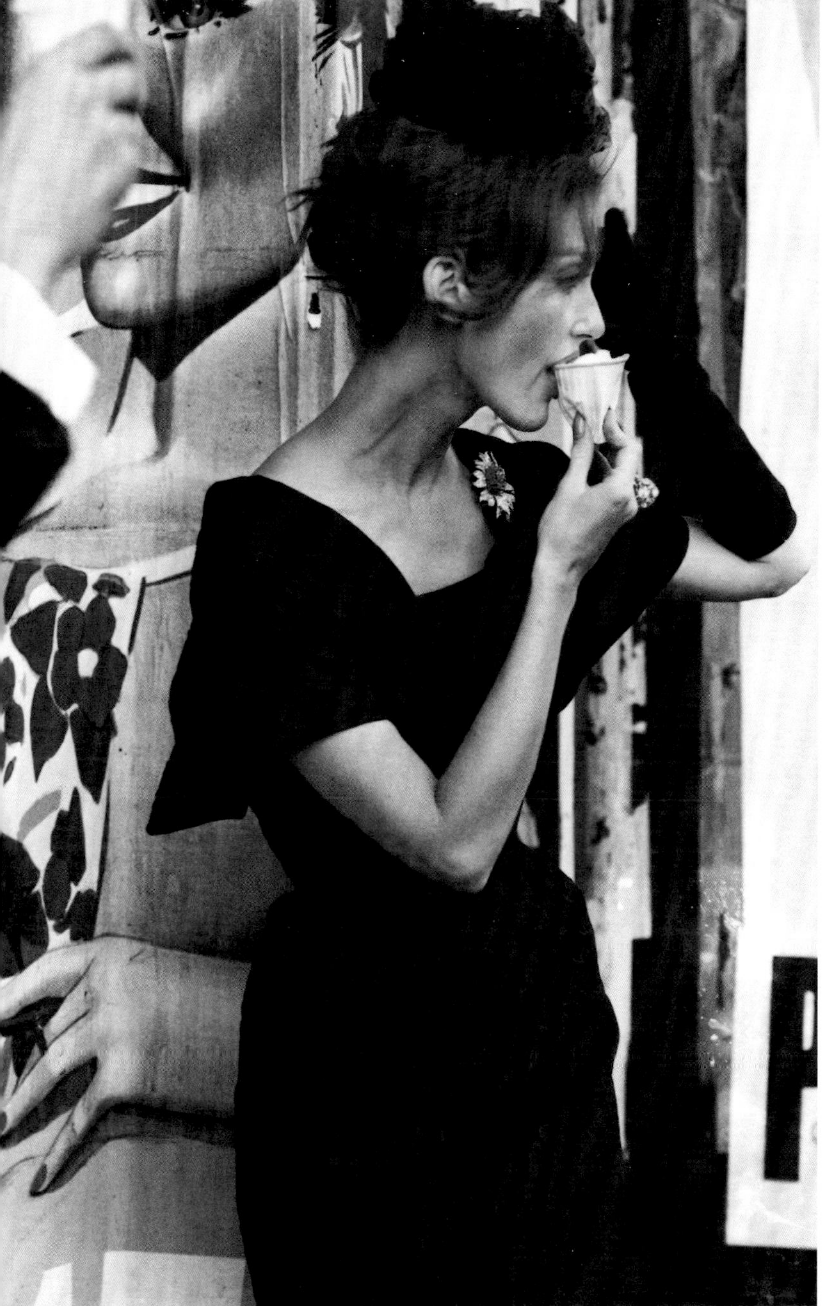

61. Tilly (for *Harper's Bazaar*), January 1964.

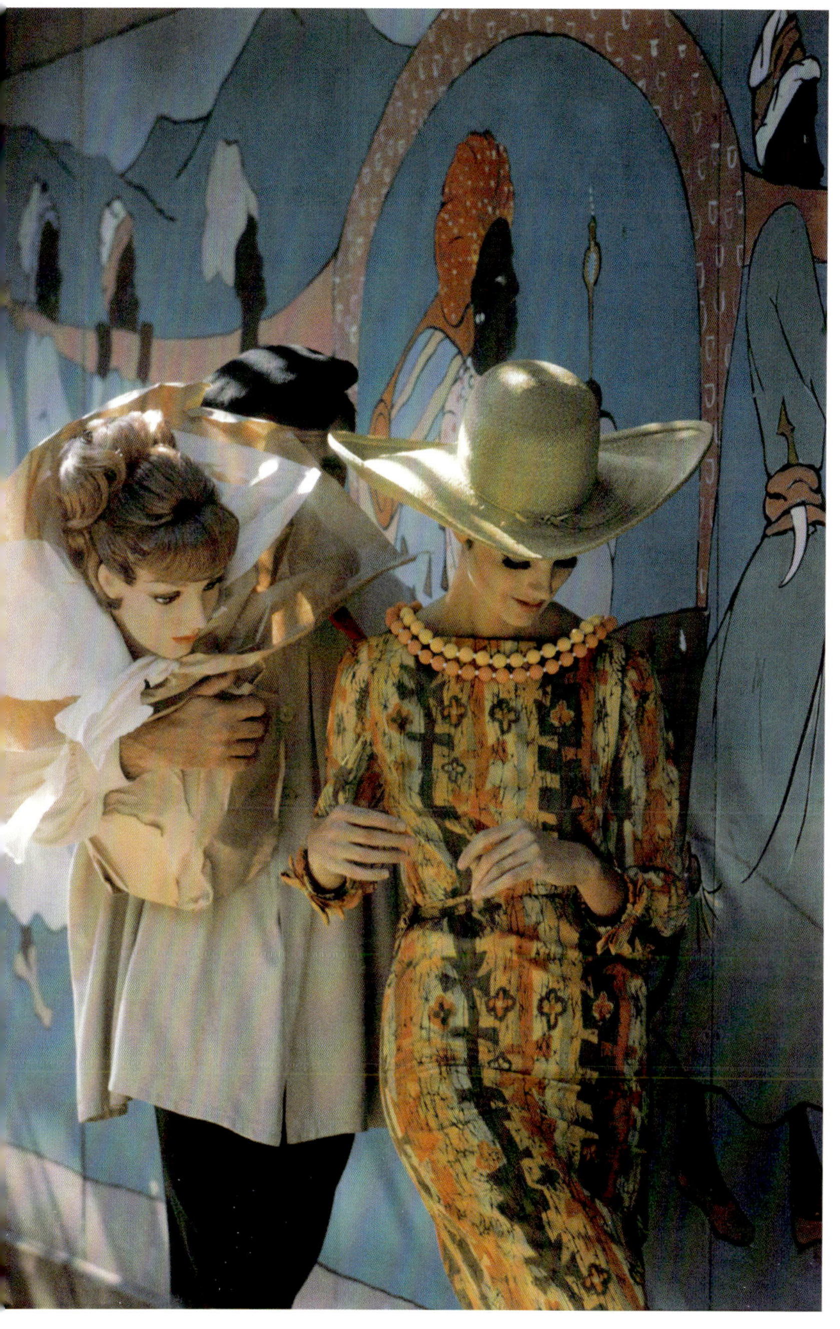

62. Untitled, undated.

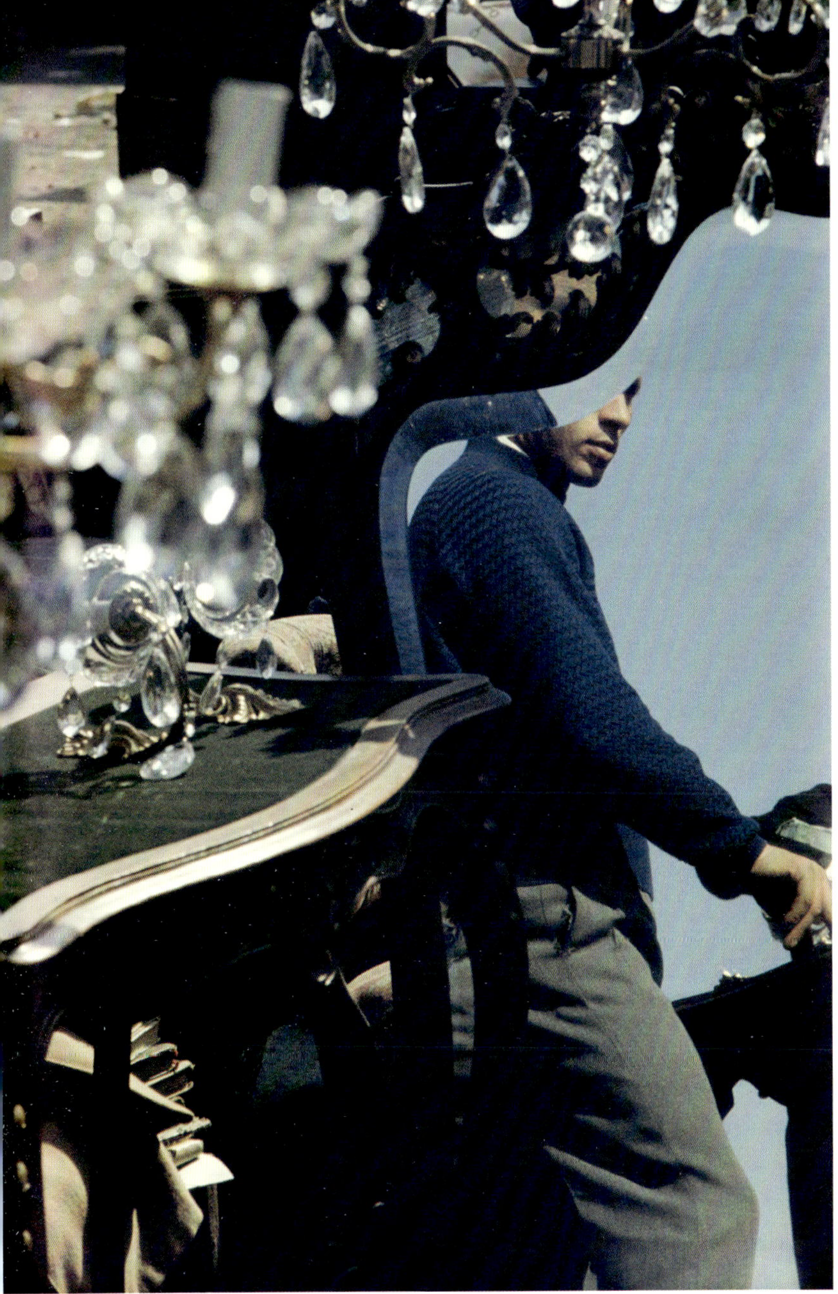

63. Untitled, undated.

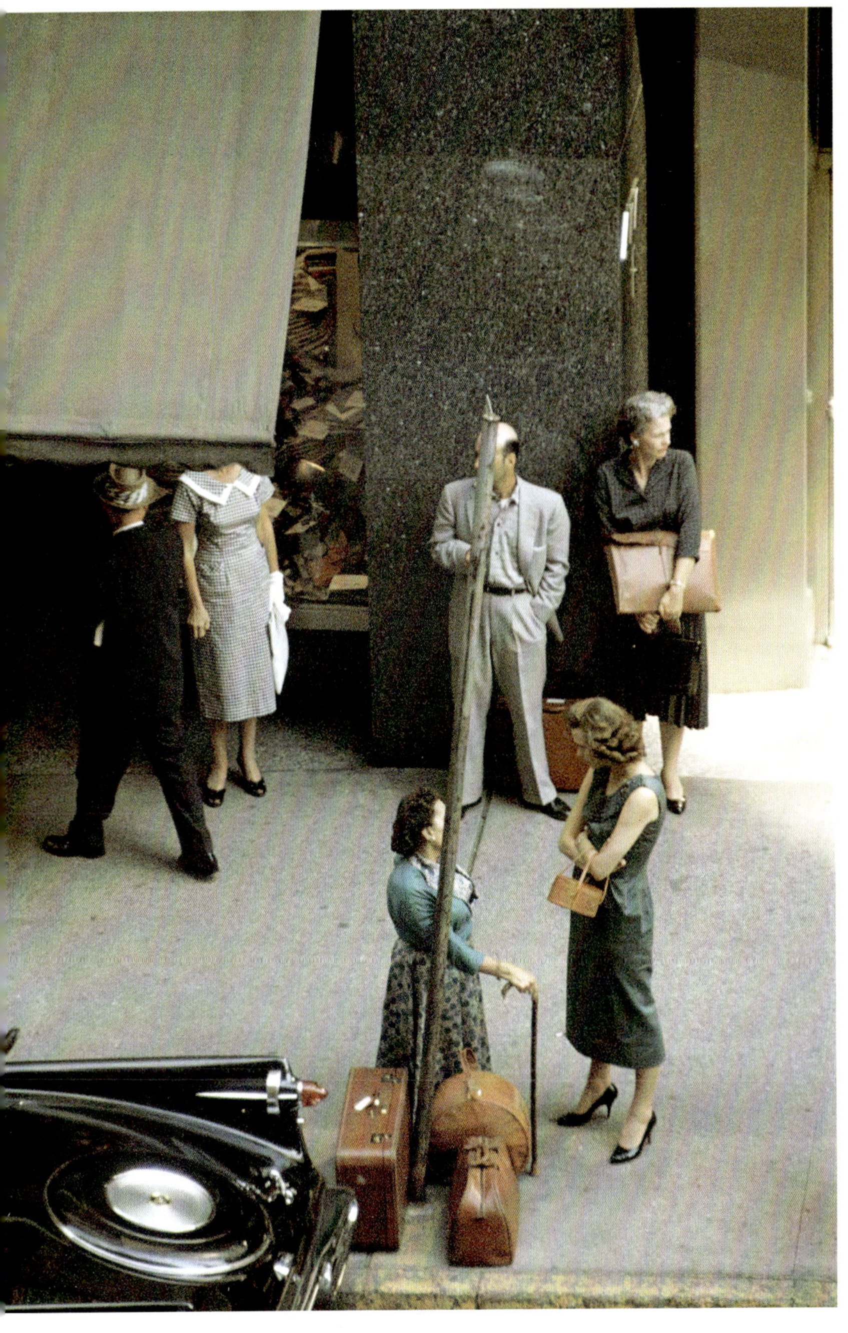

64. Untitled (Lanesville), 1958

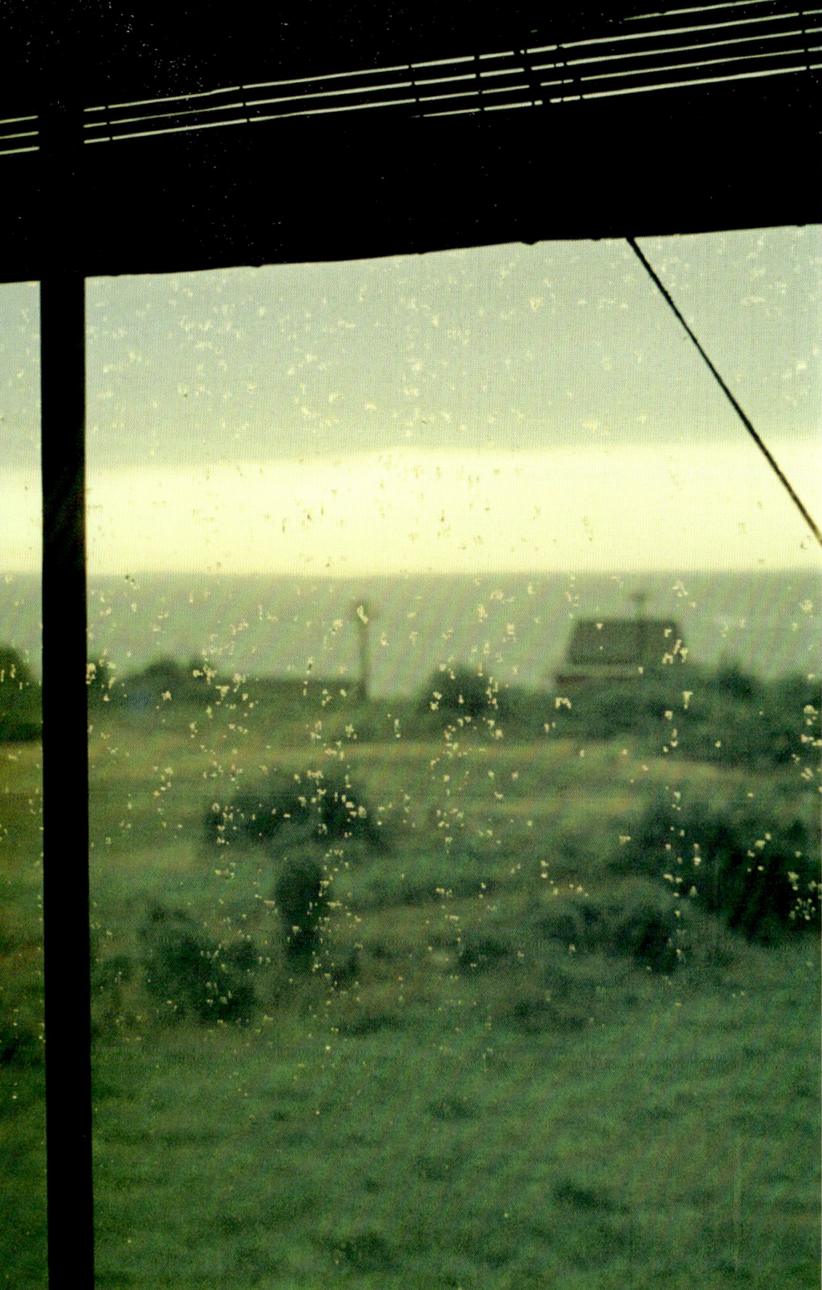

Biography

1923 Born in Pittsburgh, Pennsylvania.

1930s Attends Talmudical Academy in New York City.

1935 Is given a Detrola camera by his mother and begins photographing sporadically.

1940s Leiter attends Telshe Yeshiva Rabbinical College in Cleveland, Ohio.

1944 Paintings exhibited at Ten Thirty Gallery, Cleveland, Ohio.

1945 Paintings exhibited at The Outlines Gallery, Pittsburgh.

1946 Leaves theological college in Cleveland and moves to New York. Meets abstract expressionist painter Richard Pousette-Dart, who influences his interest in photography.

1947 Attends Henri Cartier-Bresson's exhibition at the Museum of Modern Art, New York. One of Leiter's paintings is included in *Abstract and Surrealist American Art* at the Art Institute of Chicago. Meets and befriends W. Eugene Smith, who gives him Alexey Brodovitch's book *Ballet*. Leiter's paintings are exhibited at the Butler Institute of American Art, Youngstown, Ohio.

1948 Begins working with color slide film. Works primarily with three cameras: an Argosy C3, an Auto Graflex Junior, and an early Rolleiflex.

1951 *Life* publishes his series "The Wedding as a Funeral" and "Shoes of the Shoeshine Man."

1952 Moves to East 10th Street. Founding of the cooperative Tanager Gallery.

1953 His black-and-white photographs are included in *Always the Young Strangers* at MoMA, New York, and in *Contemporary Photography* at the Tokyo Museum.

1954 Marries Barbara Hatch in Port Chester, New York, on May 29.

1957 Some of his color work is included in the slide talk "Experimental Photography in Color" and the exhibition *Photographs from the Museum Collection* at the Museum of Modern Art, New York, organized by Edward Steichen.

1958 Begins to work for *Harper's Bazaar* when Henry Wolf becomes art director.

1959 Travels to Madrid on assignment for *Esquire* to photograph Gina Lollobrigida during the making of *Solomon and Sheba*.

late 1950s Gives slide talk about his color work at The Club, an art space in the East Village.

1960–1962 Rents a studio from fashion photographer John Rawlings. Meets the model Soames Bantry (Judith Vaughan) from Redding, Connecticut, who moves into 111 East 10th Street with him.

1960–1980s Alongside his commercial work, he continues to do fashion photography, which is published in *Harper's Bazaar, Elle, Show, Vogue* (UK), *Queen*, and *Nova*. His photographs are also included in *Life, US Camera, Photography Annual*, and *Infinity*. Travels to Mexico, France, Italy, and Israel.

1981 Closes his commercial studio at 156 5th Avenue, New York.

1993 Receives funding from Ilford Paper Company to begin printing color work as Cibachromes with Laumont Labs in New York.

1997 Exhibitions of color photographs at Howard Greenberg Gallery, New York.

2002 Gives talk at the Jewish Museum, New York, to coincide with the exhibition *New York: Capital of Photography*. Soames Bantry dies on October 9.

2006 First solo museum exhibition at the Milwaukee Art Museum. Attends exhibition and gives talk.

2008 First solo museum show in Europe at the Fondation Henri Cartier-Bresson, Paris, with accompanying book. Gives talk and slide show at the Jewish Museum, Paris.

2009 First painting exhibition in over thirty years at Knoedler Gallery, New York.

2010 Travels to Berlin to give talk and slide show at C/O Berlin.

2013 Dies on November 26 at his home in New York's East Village where he has lived for sixty years.

2014 Creation of the Saul Leiter Foundation, with the aim of preserving the art and legacy of Saul Leiter and promoting the appreciation, advancement, and conservation of photographic works worldwide.

Selected Bibliography

Saul Leiter: Early Color, text by Martin Harrison, Göttingen: Steidl, 2006; 2nd ed. 2008; 3rd ed. 2011; 4th ed. 2013

In Living Color: Photographs by Saul Leiter, text by Lisa Hostetler, Milwaukee: Milwaukee Art Museum, 2006

Saul Leiter: Early Black and White, text by Martin Harrison, Göttingen: Steidl, 2008; 2nd ed. 2013

Saul Leiter, text by Agnès Sire, Göttingen: Steidl, 2008

Saul Leiter: Photofile, London: Thames & Hudson, 2008

Saul Leiter, Dancing in the Street, Chalon-sur-Saône: Musée Nicéphore Niépce, 2009

Saul Leiter: Painted Photographs, Göttingen: Steidl, 2012

Saul Leiter: Sketchbook #1, Göttingen: Steidl, 2012

Saul Leiter: Retrospective, eds. Brigitte Woischnik and Ingo Taubhorn, Hamburg: Kehrer Verlag, 2012

Saul Leiter: Early Black and White, ed. Max Kozloff, New York: Howard Greenberg Gallery; Göttingen: Steidl, 2014

Saul Leiter: Painted Nudes, London: Sylph Editions, 2015

Fashion Eye: New York, text by Martin Harrison, Paris: Louis Vuitton, 2017

It Don't Mean a Thing, text by Paul Auster, New York: Gould Collection, 2017

Saul Leiter: In My Room, text by Carole Naggar & Robert Benton, Göttingen: Steidl, 2017

The Ballad of Soames Bantry, text by Michael Torosian, Toronto: Lumiere Press, 2017

All About Saul Leiter, text by Pauline Vermare, Margit Erb & Motoyuki Shibata, London: Thames & Hudson, 2018

Saul Leiter: East 10th Street, text by Roger Szmulewicz, Antwerp: Fifty One, 2018

Saul Leiter: Women, text by Michael Parillo, Tokyo: Space Shower Books, 2018

Forever Saul Leiter, text by Akiko Otake, Margit Erb & Michael Parillo, Tokyo: Shogakukan, 2020

Saul Leiter: Painted Nudes, text by Mona Gainer-Salim, London: Sylph Editions, 2015

All About Saul Leiter, text by Margit Erb, Motoyuki Shibata and Pauline Vermare, Kyoto: Seigensha Art Publishing; Paris: Textuel; London: Thames & Hudson, 2018

Forever Saul Leiter, text by Margit Erb, Michael Parillo and Akiko Otake, Tokyo: Shogakukan; London: Thames & Hudson; Paris: Textuel, 2021

Saul Leiter, text by Michael Parillo, Paju-si: Youlhwadang, 2022

The Unseen Saul Leiter, text by Margit Erb and Michael Parillo, London: Thames & Hudson; Paris: Textuel, 2022

Saul Leiter: The Centennial Retrospective, text by Adam Harrison Levy, Michael Greenberg, Lou Stoppard, Asa Hiramatsu and Margit Erb, London: Thames & Hudson, 2023

Selected Exhibitions

Solo exhibitions

1944 Ten Thirty Gallery, Cleveland, OH.
1945 The Outlines Gallery, Pittsburgh, PA.
1947 Butler Institute of American Art, Youngstown, OH.
1950s Tanager Gallery, New York.
1972 Midtown Y, New York.
1984 Gallery Lafayette, New York.
1985 Gallery Lafayette, New York.
1993 Howard Greenberg Gallery, New York.
1994 Howard Greenberg Gallery, New York.
1997 *Saul Leiter: In Color*, Howard Greenberg Gallery, New York; Martha Schneider Gallery, Chicago.
2004 *Saul Leiter: In Color*, Staton-Greenberg Gallery, Santa Barbara, CA.
2005 *Saul Leiter: Early Color*, Howard Greenberg Gallery, New York.
2006 *In Living Color: Photographs by Saul Leiter*, Milwaukee Art Museum, WI.
– *Saul Leiter: Color*, Fifty One Fine Art Photography, Antwerp.
– *The Fashion Photographs of Saul Leiter*, Festival International de Mode et de Photographie, Hyères, France.
2007 *Saul Leiter: Early Color*, University of Maine Museum of Art, Bangor, ME.
2008 *Saul Leiter*, Fondation Henri Cartier-Bresson, Paris.
– *Saul Leiter*, Galleria Carla Sozzani, Milan.
– *Saul Leiter*, Jackson Fine Art, Atlanta.
– *Saul Leiter Women*, Howard Greenberg Gallery, New York.
– *Saul Leiter*, Faggionato Fine Arts, London.
– *Saul Leiter*, Galerie Camera Obscura, Paris.
2009 *Saul Leiter Paintings*, Knoedler Gallery, New York.
– *Saul Leiter*, Fifty One Fine Art Photography, Antwerp.
– *Saul Leiter*, Nicole Stanner Gallery, Munich.
– *Saul Leiter*, Musée Nicéphore Niépce, Chalon-sur-Saône, France.
2010 *Saul Leiter*, Gallery.ru, Moscow.
– *Saul Leiter: Photographs & Paintings*, Galerie Camera Obscura, Paris.
– *Saul Leiter Paintings*, KMR Arts, Washington Depot, CT.
2011 *Saul Leiter*, Musée de l'Elysée, Lausanne.
– *Saul Leiter*, Jewish Historical Museum, Amsterdam.
2012 *Saul Leiter*, Deichtorhallen, Hamburg.
– *Saul Leiter*, Forma Foundation for Photography, Milan.
– *Saul Leiter*, Nicholas Metivier Gallery, Toronto.
2013 *Saul Leiter*, Fifty One Fine Art Photography, Antwerp.
– *Saul Leiter: A Life in Colour*, HackelBury Fine Art, London.
– *Saul Leiter: Early Colors*, Museo Cantonale d'Arte, Lugano, Switzerland.
– *Saul Leiter: Post-War Color*, Rose Gallery, Santa Monica, CA.
– *Saul Leiter*, Kunsthaus, Vienna.
2014 *Saul Leiter. Retrospektive*, Fotografie Forum Frankfurt.
– *Saul Leiter: Early Black and White*, Howard Greenberg Gallery, New York.
2015 *Saul Leiter: Early Black and White*, Fifty One Fine Art Photography, Antwerp.
2016 *Saul Leiter: Retrospektive*, FOMU, Antwerp.
– *Saul Leiter: Retrospective*, The Photographers' Gallery, London.
2017 *Photographer Saul Leiter: A Retrospective*, Bunkamura Museum of Art, Tokyo.
2018 *Photographer Saul Leiter: A Retrospective*, Itami City Museum, Japan.
– *Saul Leiter: In Search of Beauty*, Fundació Foto Colectania, Barcelona.
– *Saul Leiter: In My Room*, Howard Greenberg Gallery, New York.
2019 *Saul Leiter. Retrospektive*, Kunstfoyer, Munich.
– *Photographer Saul Leiter: A Retrospective*, Bandaijima Art Museum, Niigata, Japan.
2020 *Forever Saul Leiter*, Bunkamura Museum of Art, Tokyo.

Group exhibitions

1947 *Abstract and Surrealist Art*, Art Institute of Chicago.

1953 *Contemporary Photography*, Tokyo Museum, Tokyo.
– *Always the Young Strangers*, Museum of Modern Art, New York.
1980 *Fashion Photographers*, Hastings/Rinhart Galleries, New York.
1991 *Appearances: Fashion Photography since 1945*, Victoria & Albert Museum, London.
2002 *New York: Capital of Photography*, The Jewish Museum, New York.
– *New York Scene: Ted Croner, Sid Grossman, Saul Leiter and Leon Levinstein*, Howard Greenberg Gallery, New York.
2006 *Color Photography*, Amon Carter Museum, Fort Worth, TX.
– *The Streets of New York*, National Gallery of Art, Washington DC.
2009 *In the Darkroom*, National Gallery of Art, Washington DC.
– *Recent Acquisitions*, Maison Européenne de la Photographie, Paris.
2012 *Cartier-Bresson: A Question of Colour*, Positive View Foundation, London.
– *New York in Color*, Howard Greenberg Gallery, New York.
– *Saul Leiter, Evelyn Hofer, Raghubir Singh*, Galerie f5.6, Munich.
2013 *Color Rush: 75 Years of Color Photography*, Milwaukee Art Museum, WI.
– *Convergence*, HackelBury Fine Art, London.
2019 *Saul Leiter, David Lynch, Helmut Newton: Nudes*, Helmut Newton Foundation, Berlin.
2021 *Modern Look: Photography and the American Magazine*, The Jewish Museum, New York.

The Photofile series is the original English-language edition of the Photo Poche collection. It was first published between 1986 and 1992 by the Centre National de la Photographie, Paris, with the support of the French Ministry of Culture. Robert Delpire (1926–2017) was the creator of the series and its managing editor until 2017.

General editor: Géraldine Lay

Series design by Matthew Young

First published in the United Kingdom in 2008 by
Thames & Hudson Ltd, 6-24 Britannia Street, London WC1X 9JD

First published in the United States of America in 2009 by
Thames & Hudson Inc., 500 Fifth Avenue, New York, New York 10110

Revised edition first published 2023

Reprinted 2025

EU Authorized Representative: Interart S.A.R.L.
19 rue Charles Auray, 93500 Pantin, Paris, France
productsafety@thameshudson.co.uk
www.interart.fr

The interior paper used in this book is PEFC-certified. This book is printed entirely on paper from sustainably managed forests.

A CIP catalogue record for this book is available from the British Library

Library of Congress Control Number 2023934217

ISBN 978-0-500-29768-1
02

Printed and bound in Italy